# ICFA Continuing Education
# Finding Reality in Reported Earnings

Proceedings of the AIMR seminar *Finding Reality in Reported Earnings*

December 4, 1996
Philadelphia, Pennsylvania

E. Richard Brownlee III
Martin S. Fridson, CFA
Trevor S. Harris
David F. Hawkins

Patricia A. McConnell
Fred H. Speece, Jr., CFA, *Moderator*
Kathryn F. Staley, CFA
Robert Willens

Edited by Jan R. Squires, CFA

To obtain the *AIMR Publications Catalog*, contact:
AIMR, P.O. Box 3668, Charlottesville, Virginia 22903, U.S.A.
Phone 804-980-3668; Fax 804-980-9755; E-mail info@aimr.org
or
visit AIMR's World Wide Web site at **www.aimr.org**
to view the AIMR publications list.

©1997, Association for Investment Management and Research

All rights reserved. No part of this publication may be reproduced, stored in a retrieval system, or transmitted, in any form or by any means, electronic, mechanical, photocopying, recording, or otherwise, without prior written permission of the copyright holder.

*ICFA Continuing Education* is published monthly seven times a year in March, April, May, May, July, September, and November by the Association for Investment Management and Research, P.O. Box 3668, Charlottesville, Virginia 22903, U.S.A. This publication is designed to provide accurate and authoritative information with regard to the subject matter covered. It is sold with the understanding that the publisher is not engaged in rendering legal, accounting, or other professional services. If legal advice or other expert assistance is required, the services of a competent professional should be sought. Periodicals postage paid at the post office in Richmond, Virginia, and additional mailing offices.

Copies are mailed as a benefit of membership to CFA® charterholders. Subscriptions also are available at US$100 for one year. Address all circulation communications to ICFA Continuing Education, P.O. Box 3668, Charlottesville, Virginia 22903, U.S.A.; Phone 804-980-3668; Fax 804-980-9755. For change of address, send mailing label and new address six weeks in advance.

Postmaster: Send address changes to the Association for Investment Management and Research, P.O. Box 3668, Charlottesville, Virginia 22903.

ISBN 1-879087-84-7
Printed in the United States of America
May 1997

### Editorial Staff

Charlene Semer
*Editor*

Jaynee M. Dudley
*Production Manager*

Marsha Gainey
*Assistant Editor*

Diane B. Hamshar
*Typesetting/Layout*

# Contents

Foreword .................................................................... v
   Katrina F. Sherrerd, CFA

Biographies of Speakers ..................................................... vi

Finding Reality in Reported Earnings: An Overview ........................... 1
   Jan R. Squires, CFA

Communicating Corporate Value: The Role of Financial Reporting .............. 4
   E. Richard Brownlee II

The Subtleties of Reporting Earnings ....................................... 12
   Martin S. Fridson, CFA

Searching for Real Earnings: Practical Suggestions ......................... 23
   Kathryn F. Staley, CFA

Reported Earnings for Multinational Corporations: The Impact of Currency Translation .... 32
   Trevor S. Harris

Understanding Global Accounting Practices and Standards .................... 40
   David F. Hawkins

Accounting for Business Combinations and Restructurings .................... 46
   Patricia A. McConnell

The Effect of Taxes on Reported Earnings ................................... 57
   Robert Willens

Self-Evaluation Examination
   Questions .............................................................. 64
   Answers ................................................................ 66

Selected Publications ...................................................... 68

## ICFA Board of Trustees, 1996–97

Frank K. Reilly, CFA, *Chair*
Notre Dame, Indiana

Fred H. Speece, Jr., CFA, *Vice Chair*
Minneapolis, Minnesota

I. Rossa O'Reilly, CFA, *AIMR Chair*
Toronto, Ontario, Canada

Abby Joseph Cohen, CFA, *AIMR Vice Chair*
New York, New York

Thomas A. Bowman, CFA, *AIMR President and CEO*
Charlottesville, Virginia

Edmund D. Kellogg, CFA
Boston, Massachusetts

George W. Long, CFA
Hong Kong

Thomas P. Moore, Jr., CFA
Boston, Massachusetts

George W. Noyes, CFA*
Boston, Massachusetts

Lee N. Price, CFA
San Francisco, California

Philippe A. Sarasin, CFA
Geneva, Switzerland

Brian F. Wruble, CFA
New York, New York

*ex officio*

## AIMR Education Committee, 1996–97

Frank K. Reilly, CFA, *Chair*
Notre Dame, Indiana

Fred H. Speece, Jr., CFA, *Vice Chair*
Minneapolis, Minnesota

Terry L. Arndt, CFA
Mount Pleasant, Michigan

Thomas A. Bowman, CFA
Charlottesville, Virginia

Keith C. Brown, CFA
Austin, Texas

Abby Joseph Cohen, CFA
New York, New York

Scott L. Lummer, CFA
Chicago, Illinois

Charles F. O'Connell, CFA
Chicago, Illinois

I. Rossa O'Reilly, CFA
Toronto, Ontario, Canada

Katrina F. Sherrerd, CFA
Charlottesville, Virginia

J. Clay Singleton, CFA
Charlottesville, Virginia

R. Charles Tschampion, CFA
New York, New York

## AIMR Senior Education Staff

Thomas A. Bowman, CFA
*President* and *CEO*

Katrina F. Sherrerd, CFA
*Senior Vice President*

J. Clay Singleton, CFA
*Senior Vice President*

Terence E. Burns, CFA
*Vice President*

Julia S. Hammond, CFA
*Vice President*

Robert R. Johnson, CFA
*Vice President*

Robert M. Luck, Jr., CFA
*Vice President*

Aaron L. Shackelford, CFA
*Vice President*

Donald L. Tuttle, CFA
*Vice President*

Barbara L. Higgins
*Director*

Paul W. Turner
*Director*

# Foreword

The figures that companies report in their financial statements as their interim or annual earnings assume great significance in the eyes of financial analysts and the financial press. Movements in these earnings data are interpreted widely as symptomatic of a company's health and growth. Many studies have shown that better (or worse) than expected earnings reports have an important buoying (depressing) influence on stock price. Therefore, companies have every incentive to issue optimistic earnings statements.

The principal question under discussion in this proceedings is the extent to which these earnings reports are real and the extent to which they are fantasy—the invention of a clever management. How is it possible to manipulate earnings figures without losing credibility? How can analysts spot telltale discrepancies in the financial accounts that signal the presence of something questionable? Although accounting practices are regulated, what might the accounts legitimately conceal? What questions to management might elicit a truer picture of the company's status? What is the meaning of earnings figures from non-U.S. companies, and how do they compare with those from U.S. companies?

The speakers at AIMR's conference, "Finding Reality in Reported Earnings," held in Philadelphia on December 4, 1996, are experienced and adept at reading between the lines of public financial statements to discover the true state of a company's present health and future prospects. The presentations in this proceedings offer wary analysts sound insights and advice on the subtleties of how the earnings game is played.

We wish to thank Fred H. Speece, Jr., CFA, of Speece, Lewis & Thorson for acting as moderator for this seminar. We would also like to thank the seminar's speakers for their valuable participation: E. Richard Brownlee II, University of Virginia Darden Graduate School of Business; Martin S. Fridson, CFA, Merrill Lynch & Company; Trevor S. Harris, Columbia University; David F. Hawkins, Harvard University Graduate School of Business; Patricia A. McConnell, Bear, Stearns & Company; Kathryn F. Staley, CFA, Gilder, Gagnon, Howe & Company; and Robert Willens, Lehman Brothers.

Katrina F. Sherrerd, CFA
Senior Vice President
Educational Products

# Biographies of Speakers

**E. Richard Brownlee II** is professor of business administration at the Darden Graduate School of Business Administration at the University of Virginia. Previously, he was affiliated with KPMG Peat Marwick and served as a consultant to the Institute of Chartered Financial Analysts. Professor Brownlee has authored or co-authored various books and case studies on financial accounting and reporting. A *Management Accounting* article, "Capitalizing on Excess Pension Assets," won the William Lybrand Gold Medal Award from the Institute of Management Accountants in 1986. He holds a B.B.A. and an M.B.A. from Ohio University and a Ph.D. from Georgia State University.

**Martin S. Fridson, CFA,** is chief high-yield strategist at Merrill Lynch & Company. He serves on the editorial boards of the *Financial Analysts Journal, Financial Management,* and *The CFA Digest* and is past president of the Fixed Income Analysts Society. Mr. Fridson has been selected by *Institutional Investor* for its list of "The Next Generation of Financial Leaders" and for its All-America Research Team. In addition to numerous articles, he has written several books, including *Investment Illusions—A Savvy Wall Street Pro Explodes Popular Misconceptions about the Markets,* (John Wiley & Sons, 1996), *Financial Statement Analysis: A Practitioner's Guide,* 2nd ed. (John Wiley & Sons, 1996), and *High Yield Bonds: Identifying Value and Assessing Risk of Speculative Grade Securities* (Irwin Professional Publishing, 1989). Mr. Fridson holds a B.A. in history from Harvard College and an M.B.A. from Harvard Business School.

**Trevor S. Harris** is the Kester and Byrnes Professor of Accounting and Auditing at Columbia Business School. He teaches in both full-time and executive programs and consults on active research, accounting, and valuation issues for Salomon Brothers and TIAA-CREF and on international accounting issues for the NYSE. Previously, he was a vice president at Salomon Brothers, local manager of Arthur Andersen & Company in Cape Town, South Africa, and a visiting accounting professor at the University of Chicago. Professor Harris is a chartered accountant and a member of the AIMR Financial Accounting Practices Committee; and the consultant committee of the International Accounting Standards Committee. He is the recipient of the Singhui award for teaching excellence at Columbia Business School. Professor Harris has written articles and a book titled *International Accounting Standards vs. U.S.-GAAP: Empirical Evidence Based on Case Studies* (South-Western Publishing Company, 1995). He holds an M.Comm. from the University of Cape Town, South Africa, and a Ph.D. from the University of Washington.

**David F. Hawkins** is a professor at the Harvard University Graduate School of Business Administration in the fields of accounting and finance. He is also the accounting consultant to Merrill Lynch & Company's global equity and fixed-income research groups. He was named a first team member on *Institutional Investor's* 1990 All-America Team in the accounting category. Professor Hawkins is the author or co-author of numerous articles and books, including *Corporate Financial Reporting: Text and Analysis* (Irwin, 1997) and *Equity Valuation: Models, Analysis, and Implications: A Research Study and Report* (Financial Executives Research Foundation, 1992).

**Patricia A. McConnell** is senior managing director of Bear, Stearns & Company. She specializes in accounting and taxation applied to investment banking transactions and institutional security analysis. Ms. McConnell has been named to *Institutional Investor's* All-America Research Team of financial analysts for the past seven years. She is a member of the Board of Governors of AIMR, past chair of the Financial Accounting Policies Committee of AIMR, a director at large of the New York Society of Security Analysts, a member of the Financial Accounting Standards Board's Financial Instruments Project Task Force, and a member of the International Accounting Standards Board. She holds an M.Ph. in economics and an M.B.A. from the Leonard N. Stern School of Business at New York University.

**Fred H. Speece, Jr., CFA,** is a founder of the investment management firm Speece, Lewis & Thorson. Previously, he was director and chair of the equity group at First Asset Management and head of trust investment at Illinios National Bank. He is on the Board of Governors of AIMR, is vice chair of the Institute of Chartered Financial Analysts, a trustee of the Research Foundation of the ICFA, and chair of the Board of Regents of the Financial Analysts Seminar. Mr. Speece holds a B.B.A. from Ohio Univeristy and an M.B.A. from Western Michigan University.

**Kathryn F. Staley, CFA,** is an analyst and portfolio manager at Gilder, Gagnon, Howe & Company. Her responsibilities include following 200 stocks in long and short positions and overseeing a small group of analysts. Prior to her current association, Ms. Staley was an analyst at Kynikos Associates, a money management firm that specializes in short selling. She is the author of *When Stocks Crash Nicely: The Fine Art of Short Selling* (Harper Business, 1991). Ms. Staley received an M.A. in English from the University of Virginia and an M.B.A. from the University of North Carolina at Chapel Hill.

**Robert Willens** is a managing director with Lehman Brothers. Prior to joining Lehman, he was tax partner in charge of the capital markets group at KPMG Peat Marwick in New York. He advises Lehman's investment banking, equity derivatives, and fixed-income departments, in addition to the firm's institutional and retail sales forces, on all manner of tax and accounting issues. Mr. Willens serves as chair of the American Institute of Certified Public Accountants committee on revision of the corporate tax laws. He has also chaired the New York State Society of Certified Public Accountants committee on distributions, liquidations, and reorganizations. Mr. Willens is the author of *Taxation of Corporate Capital Transactions: A Guide for Corporate Investment Banking and Tax Advisers* (John Wiley & Sons, 1984) and has written more than 200 articles for various publications. He is a contributing editor to the *Journal of Accountancy* and the *Journal of Taxation of Investments* and serves on the editorial board of the *Journal of Accountancy*. He was named to *Institutional Investor's* 1996 All-America Research Team. Mr. Willens is also an adjunct professor of finance at Columbia University School of Business.

# Finding Reality in Reported Earnings: An Overview

Jan R. Squires, CFA
*Professor of Finance*
*Southwest Missouri State University*

Many and varied are the tools of modern investment management—from elegant asset-pricing theories and sophisticated computers to mammoth databases and intricate optimizers. For many if not most investment practitioners, however, the most pervasive tool is also one of the most traditional: a company's financial statements. No single item on those statements commands more attention, invites more scrutiny, and attracts more controversy than reported earnings.

## REPORTED EARNINGS

Reported earnings command our attention simply because earnings, presumably, are the basis for the investment benefits that we all seek. "Healthy earnings equal healthy investment benefits" seems a logical equation, but earnings are also a scorecard by which we compare companies, a filter through which we assess management, and a crystal ball in which we try to foretell future performance. A single value that serves so many purposes invites our scrutiny. What are the components of a company's reported earnings? Are the components, and the result, real or illusory? Fleeting or permanent? Actual or desired? Stable or volatile? What is the nature of the relationship, if any, between reported earnings and stock price? A value that must satisfy so many questions inevitably attracts controversy. From the perspective of economic reality, reported earnings are largely fictional, some argue. Another oft-voiced critique is that financial statements are subject to so many manipulations that reported earnings, although not fictional, are largely meaningless as a determinant, or even a suggestion, of investment benefits.

This proceedings is the product of an AIMR seminar intended to give participants an opportunity to focus anew their attention on reported earnings—to scrutinize the always complex and often subtle composition of reported earnings and to weigh the controversies inherent in relying on reported earnings. The authors—a blend of astute academics and seasoned practitioners—bring their considerable talents to a pragmatic and honest assessment of three major influences on the nature and usefulness of reported earnings.

■ *Accounting influences*. How do prevailing accounting standards, and the rule-making bodies that promulgate those standards, influence reported earnings? To what extent do accounting and reporting practices contribute to the subtleties of reported earnings? What processes can be helpful in evaluating reported financial information?

■ *Global influences*. What are the effects of multiple currencies on the financial statements of multinational companies? How do accounting practices differ outside the United States? How are future international accounting standards likely to evolve?

■ *Specific influences*. To what extent do reported earnings reflect prevalent accounting guidelines and practices in business combinations and restructurings? What are the key differences between reported earnings and taxable earnings, and what tax considerations most influence reported earnings?

## ACCOUNTING INFLUENCES

Reported earnings are generated in the context of accounting rules and standards; understanding the influence of those rules and standards helps prevent misplaced reliance on the quality of reported earnings.

Richard Brownlee outlines key changes in the financial reporting environment and details how financial statement objectives and the Financial Accounting Standards Board have responded to those changes. Brownlee contends that accounting is a necessary but not sufficient component of the effort to communicate corporate value globally, pointing to many examples of how accounting does not, and perhaps cannot, convey fully a company's economic reality and reminding us that the link between reported earnings and stock price is tenuous at best. He closes with an intriguing look at the future of financial reporting, touching on reporting practices, investor communications, and the emerging issue of "global sustainability."

Building on the perhaps controversial assertion that the purpose of a company's financial reporting is to obtain cheap capital, Martin Fridson examines many of the earnings subtleties with which investment professionals must contend on a daily basis. He ranges across a variety of industries—from savings and loan banks and restaurant franchises to investment banks and home supplies retailers—to provide examples of manipulative accounting and questionable reporting. Shuttling cash in place of earnings, using questionable assumptions, and ignoring timing realities—all come under Fridson's skeptical eye. He also discusses several common earnings management techniques and identifies those financial ratios, all too familiar in nature but all too rarely calculated, that he believes are most helpful in detecting typical earnings distortions.

Kathryn Staley takes the perspective of a portfolio manager who is attempting to find reality in reported earnings while working on the "firing line"—with too many stocks to follow and too little time to do adequate research. Even in that daunting environment, she contends, financial statements can and do offer useful information. Staley discusses practical interpretation of earnings announcements, identifying many specific income statement and balance sheet items that are prone to manipulation and providing particularly useful insights into the proper use of conference calls. She also offers advice on key components of effective portfolio maintenance and closes with a discussion of computer databases and spreadsheets, two helpful shortcuts to make the hard work of earnings analysis more manageable.

## GLOBAL INFLUENCES

Investment professionals must increasingly rely on nondomestic reported earnings figures. The financial statements of multinationals contain frequently misinterpreted nuances, which may or may not be clarified by evolving international accounting standards.

Making economic sense of the reported earnings of multinational companies is a difficult task, and Trevor Harris provides a comprehensive look at the extent to which foreign currency considerations further complicate that task. He first illustrates the important effects on a company's reported results of foreign currency transactions and the currency translation process. He then addresses the importance of the choice of functional currency for multinational companies and examines the impact of currency translation on company analysis and valuation, in the latter regard emphasizing cash flow translation and measurement of business activity. Throughout his presentation, Harris emphasizes both the dangers of aggregate analysis of multinational companies and the importance of rigorous, fundamental analysis of the real sources of a multinational company's performance.

Recognizing that earnings analysis is increasingly taking place in a global context, David Hawkins traces the evolution of international accounting standards to their present state, focusing in particular on that evolution as it is being played out in such specific regions as the European Community and emerging markets. He elaborates on a variety of financial reporting problems that are being, or are likely to be, addressed by these evolving standards; such problems range from interim statements and segment reporting to provisions, contingencies, and disclosures, from consolidation to pooling of interests. Hawkins concludes that if the proper criteria are consistency, transparency, timeliness, and conformity, the world is indeed moving toward international accounting standards that reflect economic reality better than in the past and that, accordingly, will better serve investors.

## SPECIFIC INFLUENCES

Various specific influences leave their unique stamp on reported earnings; of particular concern to investment professionals are, first, the often arcane realm of business combinations and restructurings and, second, the ever-present effects of taxes.

Patricia McConnell addresses a variety of issues involved in accounting for business combinations and restructurings. She first presents a detailed look at the criteria that a company must meet to use pooling-of-interests accounting, focusing on particularly important requirements relating to voting stock, autonomy, independence, asset disposal, and treasury stock. She then compares and contrasts the purchase and pooling approaches, concluding that investors should not, but apparently often do, care which method is used. McConnell also discusses restructuring charges within the context of generally accepted principles of accounting income statement presentation. Discontinued operations and extraordinary items are "below the line" income statement items. Specific restructuring charges, however, may be treated differently. McConnell concludes by highlighting current requirements with respect to two common restructuring charges: the costs related to employee termination and the costs of exiting a business activity.

Taxes are an undeniable feature of whatever reality exists in reported earnings, and Robert Willens details several important tax influences, with a focus on three particularly important tasks. First, he takes a step-by-step look, using Schedule M-1 of the corporate income tax Form 1120, at the reconciliation of accounting net income with taxable net income. Second, with respect to accounting for income taxes, he examines three issues—deductible temporary differences, deferred tax assets, and the use of net operating losses for acquisition purposes—that have great potential for manipulation by a company and that often result in lack of comparability among companies. Third, Willens discusses the tax treatment, current or proposed, for several typical corporate capital transactions, including purchase accounting and "recap" accounting.

## CONCLUSION

Helping us recognize, as the authors in this proceedings do, that the gap between economic reality and reported earnings reflects varied influences is, in and of itself, a notable contribution to our professional practice. These authors know that recognition is one thing and resolution quite another, and by virtue of their experience, intellect, and conclusions, they challenge us further: How should analysts and investors proceed to understand those influences better and begin to narrow that gap? Clients deserve the best we can muster; the best as defined by the authors is clear indeed. There is no substitute for rigorous fundamental analysis—of companies and industries; of accounting rules, industry regulations, and tax laws; of the relationships among economic, financial, and valuation variables; of the practices that increasingly cross national borders. Only by such analysis, and by the hard work and persistence required to do it well, are we in a position to find the reality in reported earnings.

# Communicating Corporate Value: The Role of Financial Reporting

E. Richard Brownlee II
*Professor of Business Administration*
*Darden Graduate School of Business Administration*
*University of Virginia*

> The search for relevant reported earnings measures necessarily involves financial accounting and reporting. Such considerations range from the traditional—the evolution of accounting standards and the role of financial reporting in the valuation process—to the timely—investor communications and global sustainability.

In the search for economically relevant earnings measures, a fundamental issue is the role of financial accounting and reporting in the equity valuation process. A large body of research demonstrates that accounting numbers, particularly earnings, have information content. This same research, however, also suggests that earnings explain only a small fraction of the total variation in stock returns. Thus, although reported earnings have investment implications, they represent but one of several relevant contemporary valuation considerations. This presentation addresses the evolution and role of financial reporting within the broader context of communicating corporate value in a global economy.

## CHANGES IN THE FINANCIAL REPORTING ENVIRONMENT

Any assessment of the overall state of contemporary financial reporting and the role it plays in communicating corporate value should include some recognition and understanding of the substantial changes in the reporting environment that have occurred in the nearly 25 years since the Financial Accounting Standards Board (FASB) was formed.

- The proportion of shares owned by individual investors in the United States declined, and the proportion owned by institutional investors grew. According to a report by the Securities Industry Association, the percentage of stocks owned by individuals declined from 84 percent in 1965 to 71 percent in 1980 and to slightly less than 50 percent in 1992. In addition, institutional investors came to dominate activity in the market, accounting for more than two-thirds of the trading volume of common stocks in the United States.
- Free enterprise expanded with the rapid globalization of business markets and capital markets.
- Significant technological change greatly increased the amount and timeliness of financial and other business-related information available to external users.
- Tremendous growth occurred in the service sector, in which businesses rely more on soft assets than on hard assets for their long-term success.

The pace and scope of these changes have caused providers and users alike to rethink the objectives of financial statements and the mechanisms by which those objectives are achieved.

## OBJECTIVES OF FINANCIAL STATEMENTS

The 1960s generated widespread concern about the accuracy and usefulness of financial statements and the adequacy of the entire process of setting accounting standards. In response to that concern, two important task forces were formed. One led to the creation of the FASB in 1973, and the other led to a report by the American Institute of Certified Public Accountants (AICPA) in 1973. Titled "Objectives of Financial Statements," this report openly challenged the entire accounting profession to become more responsive to the needs of financial statement users. It informed the profession as to what its true mandate was, who its customers were, and what

those customers needed. The report included the following financial statement objectives:
- to provide information useful for making economic decisions;
- to provide statements of periodic earnings and of financial position to be useful for predicting, comparing, and evaluating enterprise earning power;
- to provide information useful to investors and creditors for predicting, comparing, and evaluating potential cash flows in terms of amount, timing, and related uncertainty; and
- to serve primarily those users who have limited authority, ability, or resources to obtain information and who rely on financial statements as their principal source of information about an enterprise's economic activities.

These objectives form the context by which financial accounting does or does not meet the needs of investors and analysts for economically relevant information. Context, however, is not sufficient; meeting such ambitious objectives requires widely accepted accounting and reporting standards.

## THE FASB

Since 1973, the FASB has been the designated private-sector organization responsible for establishing standards of financial accounting and reporting. Those standards govern the preparation of financial reports and are officially recognized as authoritative by the U.S. SEC and the AICPA.

The mission of the FASB is to establish and improve standards of financial accounting and reporting for the guidance and education of the public, including issuers, auditors, and users of financial information. Accounting standards are essential to the efficient functioning of the economy because decisions about the allocation of resources rely heavily on credible, concise, and understandable financial information. To accomplish its mission, the FASB acts to

- improve the usefulness of financial reporting by focusing on the primary characteristics of relevance and reliability and on the qualities of comparability and consistency;
- keep standards current to reflect changes in methods of doing business and changes in the economic environment;
- consider promptly any significant areas of deficiency in financial reporting that might be improved through the standard-setting process;
- promote the international comparability of accounting standards concurrent with improving the quality of financial reporting. This task was added to the FASB's mission in 1992, when the Board began to work closely with the International Accounting Standards Committee (IASC) in the development of international accounting standards; and
- improve the common understanding of the nature and purposes of information contained in financial reports.

An early FASB initiative was to use the AICPA report's recommendations as a basis for commencing a long-term project to identify a conceptual framework for accounting and reporting. Identifying that conceptual framework turned out to be a difficult task, and many observers contend that the FASB was only somewhat successful in establishing a framework. Yet the FASB's work did and does provide some conceptual guidance for financial reporting and corporate communications in general.

For instance, in 1978, the FASB issued its first statement of financial accounting concepts, a statement noteworthy for two key conclusions and a key observation. First, financial reporting should provide information that is useful to current and potential investors, creditors, and other users in making rational investment, credit, and similar decisions. Second, financial reporting should provide information to help current and potential investors, creditors, and other users in assessing the amounts, timing, and uncertainty of prospective cash receipts from dividends, interest, and the proceeds from the sale, redemption, or maturity of securities or loans. Perhaps most importantly, the statement argued that financial reporting is but one source of information needed by those who make decisions about business enterprises; such a perspective leads to a broader view of corporate communication, a view that necessarily involves accounting as the primary communication tool.

## CORPORATE COMMUNICATIONS AND ACCOUNTING

The late Fischer Black said:
> Accounting is a language that people within a firm can use to discuss its projects and progress with one another, and that they can use to tell outsiders what's happening in the firm without giving away too many of its secrets to competitors.[1]

Corporate communications are, almost by definition, critical elements of the valuation process. Nevertheless, such communications suffer from a variety of restrictions and limitations, not the least of which is the need for a common language with all its attendant deficiencies. As Black suggested, the common

---

[1] "Choosing Accounting Rules: Improving the Informativeness of the Earnings Figure," *Accounting Horizons*, December 1993:1–17.

language used in communications with shareholders is primarily accounting based, and accounting plays a communications role both internally and externally. Its origin dates back 500 years to the development of a double-entry recordkeeping system by Renaissance merchants in order to provide financial information about economic resources, owners' investments and obligations, and the profitability of business transactions. Within this historic double-entry system, much of what constitutes contemporary accounting and reporting in the United States has been shaped during the past 25 years.

Several factors make accounting a necessary and useful but not sufficient language for contemporary communication. The traditional accounting system was primarily designed for merchandising and manufacturing companies engaged in domestic businesses in an environment characterized by gradual change; their assets were largely tangible and their liabilities were largely known both in type and amount. Essentially the same model is being used to try to capture economic reality for global businesses using soft assets to provide services in a rapidly changing environment.

Timely financial reporting usually requires extensive estimates and judgments by management. Two overriding concepts typically prevail—matching and conservatism, but these two can certainly conflict. The financial reporting model attempts to achieve two primary qualities—relevance and reliability, but these two often conflict.

The underlying accounting standards are influenced by politics, personalities, special interests, and compromise. The financial reporting model is intended to present an accurate representation of the past but also meet the needs of the users whose primary interest is in forecasting the future.

From the perspective of analysts and investors, this litany of some of the limitations of accounting as a communication vehicle spawns a fair question: What is, or should be, the relationship between the valuation process and financial reporting?

## VALUATION AND FINANCIAL REPORTING

Does financial reporting information contribute positively to the valuation process? An extensive body of research reveals considerable variety in techniques and results but permits at least three general conclusions:

- First, the statistical association between earnings and stock returns has been historically weak and has declined substantially during the past 40 years.
- Second, when a broader set of financial data are used, the statistical association with stock price improves. Still, this relationship has also declined during the past 40 years.
- Third, the statistical association between earnings and stock returns is inversely related to business volatility.

Earnings play a more significant role, have much higher correlations with stock prices, when businesses are stable; the role is much reduced in periods characterized by rapid growth, high uncertainty, and many surprises.

These findings do not suggest that earnings and other financial information provided by the accounting and reporting process is not useful to analysts, but they do suggest that the valuation process is becoming increasingly complex and that the role accounting and reporting play has changed, perhaps becoming less important.

Every firm and every security has a value, although the amount represents an estimate based on incomplete and imprecise information. Only traded securities have a price. Financial analysts look for market anomalies (i.e., securities whose perceived values are different from their current prices). Analysts use a variety of approaches to determine the value of a security. Thus, even in the most efficient markets, different analysts arrive at different valuations because the value of a security represents the present value of estimated future cash flows that are *uncertain* in both amounts and timing.

The financial reporting process results in a continual assimilation of information that quickly finds its way into the market. Thus, security values are usually affected prior to the information appearing in the financial statements or footnotes. Sometimes, however, financial statements do contain surprises. Even when they do not, they may still contain information (e.g., they may simply serve as validation of prior estimates).

Value creation depends on profitable operations, and the best measure of profitability is permanent earnings of the core business or businesses. Ideally, permanent earnings could be determined so as to approximate economic earnings. Unfortunately, most businesses are far too complex and their futures are far too uncertain to permit the timely determination of economic earnings. Even in the simplest of situations, we would have different perceptions of economic earnings.

What is reality? What is meant by economic earnings? In something simple such as inventory valuation, is determination of earnings based on LIFO or is FIFO a truer representation of economic earnings? What about full costing or variable costing, not to mention more complicated issues, such as lease transactions, restructuring, stock options, and derivatives? If those in a room full of analysts (or accountants) agreed not to leave the room until they reached consensus on the economic reality of even one of these topics, the room would never empty.

Not only is economic reality difficult to capture in a timely fashion, but opinions and perceptions of economic reality can and do differ dramatically. Seeking economic reality is a useful objective and goal, but there should be no illusions that it can be captured at all, much less in quarterly financial statements.

Try for economic reality? Yes. Succeed in capturing it? Probably not, for several reasons. One of the few constants in business today is change. Markets, products, customer expectations, information technologies, and investor requirements are changing rapidly. Companies have become flatter, leaner, more productive, and more customer and shareholder focused. Change in financial reporting, however, comes slowly and has not kept pace with the changes that have occurred in business. Financial reporting standards evolve through an open process that allows much input from and deliberation by many constituents; the process is thoughtful but can be slow and even cumbersome.

This issue will continue to be an important one for the IASC as it tries to establish standards that are responsive to the pace of environmental change and to their own ambitious objectives to reduce comment and discussion time and accelerate the rate at which international standards are finalized.

Although still of considerable importance to analysts and to the efficient functioning of the securities markets, the relative usefulness of financial reports has declined during the past 35–40 years. Alternate sources of business information, such as direct communications with analysts by the chief financial officer (CFO), letters to shareholders, and home pages on the World Wide Web, have become increasingly common.

## THE FUTURE OF FINANCIAL REPORTING

Financial reporting and analysis will become more challenging as businesses become more complex and global and as international accounting standards gain acceptance. Three aspects of the future of financial reporting warrant attention by analysts and investors: specific reporting practices, investor communications policies, and global sustainability.

### Reporting Practices

Analysts and other external users would be better served through a process of "business reporting," of which financial reporting is an essential component. This idea was one of the major recommendations of the report titled "Improving Business Reporting—A Customer Focus" of the AICPA Special Committee on Financial Reporting in 1994. Business reporting should include information about strategy, opportunities, risks, and uncertainties. Much of the information provided should pertain to the future.

Greater emphasis should be placed on reporting those key factors that will create long-term value for the business, so-called "soft assets," such as global brands, strategic alliances, and customer acquisition costs. Clearly, for instance, the values of Coca-Cola Company and PepsiCo are not in their plant and equipment but in their product formulas, trademarks, and distribution channels.

Permanent earnings from core businesses will continue to be a key measure of profitability. Capturing economic reality should continue to be a primary objective. Such an objective is elusive, however, because of different perceptions of reality and significant uncertainties about the future consequences of past activities. The fact remains that capturing today's reality requires knowledge of the future.

The addition of comprehensive income to the financial reporting model would benefit external users. Comprehensive income is defined as the change in equity (i.e., net assets) of a business enterprise during a period from transactions and other events and circumstances from nonowner sources. It would allow greater mark-to-market flexibility, focus increased attention on the underlying business implications, and provide for a more meaningful presentation of a variety of income-related components.

Corporate officers must be prepared to go before the financial analyst community and communicate openly and honestly. Just as stock price will be influenced by the quality of earnings, so too will it be influenced by management credibility. Management's view of the future should be considerably clearer than what can be seen through historical financial statements.

Future stock prices will have multiple drivers, most of which are forward looking. Both industry and general economic factors will play a role, as will the assessment of reported actual results, expected future results, and the understanding and evaluation of corporate strategy, including management's ability to execute it. Finally, stock price will be influenced by management's ability to communicate its valuation message, and that ability to communicate depends a great deal on the level of trust that investors have in top management.

## Investor Communications

In *The CFO Handbook*, A. Nicholas Filippello, vice president of financial communications and chief economist of Monsanto Company, states that a sound financial communications policy is based on five basic premises:[2]

- The equities market is reasonably efficient over time.
- Fair and appropriate sustained market value will be attained only when the financial community has an accurate understanding of the markets and major conditions affecting the corporation's various businesses, of corporate and financial strategies, and of key risk and success factors.
- The optimal level of financial and other disclosure increases with the complexity and breadth of the businesses in which the corporation is engaged.
- The equity market's required rate of return for a given company will reflect confidence in and credibility of management in addition to risk factors associated with the general market, the businesses, corporate strategy, and the financial structure.
- Shareholder institutions will become increasingly active in exercising their power to influence managements and/or boards of directors. It is, therefore, in the company's interest to have well-informed shareholders.

Says Filippello:

> The most important element in attracting and retaining satisfied shareowners is financial performance. . . . However, it is also vital that investors and potential investors have a solid understanding of the corporation, its products, its markets, its strategy, its goals, and the economic forces that drive financial performance. Therefore, a positive relationship with shareholders must also include an effective communications program between the company and the financial community.

John L. Bakane, CFO of Cone Mills Corporation, concurs with this view of investor communications:

> In 1983, our company was the target of a hostile takeover attempt. To me, this was the ultimate lesson in the need for balance among the company's culture, mission, and goals, and the expectations and requirements of investors who allocate capital to the macroeconomy. As a result, I believe the high-performance CFO must be involved in defining the missions and goals of the organization, particularly from the perspective of fit with expectations of the macroeconomy. This requires the CFO to develop, maintain, and communicate a model of how the organization fits with the macroeconomy.[3]

## Global Sustainability

The investment community has not become fully aware of the risks and opportunities associated with increased environmental awareness on the part of governments, consumers, the general public, employees, and top managements. In addition, the emerging corporate interest in "sustainable development" will result in many opportunities for those businesses that take a leadership role.

James Wolfensohn, president of The World Bank, says of global sustainability,

> Thirty years ago, concern for environmental issues was restricted to small groups of scientists and activists but was effectively nonexistent from the business and financial communities. Since about the time of the Stockholm environment conference in 1972, awareness of environmental problems has become more central to the thinking of innovative industrialists. This process is now gradually spreading within the financial community as banks and other financial institutions realize they cannot ignore the implications of environmental policies and concerns for their own businesses.
>
> At The World Bank, we regard the promotion of environmentally sustainable development as one of our fundamental objectives. At the same time, we recognize that the achievement of sound environmental practices depends upon a constructive partnership between businesses and governments. We hope that we can play a useful role in promoting such partnerships and in assisting governments to put in place incentives that ensure that economic growth is, in fact, sustainable.[4]

Any form of development, sustainable or not, must be financed. What role will the accountants and analysts play as more companies seek to replace unsustainable business practices with sustainable business practices?

Accountants will experience increasing expectations from their constituents with respect to environmental accounting and reporting. Corporate market valuation requires information about environment-related business risks and opportunities, and the present accounting and reporting model is not satisfactory. Increased public interest in and awareness of the health of our environment will continue to create new risks and opportunities—some the result of new environmental regulations, some the result of customer expectations and concerns, and some the result of imaginative and innovative business practices. Accountants must take a leadership role in responding to the demand for improved environmental reporting.

*Institutional Investor* (March 1995) posed the following question: Will financial markets soon be systematically rewarding environmentally successful companies while penalizing offenders? Some market observers think so, but others contend that there is

---

[2]Mark Haskins and Benjamin Makela, editors, 2nd ed. (Burr Ridge, IL: Irwin Professional Publishing, 1996):309–24.

[3]Haskins and Makela, *The CFO Handbook*:3–15.

[4]*Financing Change* (Cambridge, MA: MIT Press, 1996):IX–X.

reason to believe that financial markets in pursuit of short-term goals undervalue environmental resources, discount the future, and favor accounting and reporting systems that do not reflect environmental risks and opportunities.

Historically, analysts have viewed environmental issues as moral and emotional ones, not as issues of particular relevance to investment decisions. Times are changing, however. Analysts and investors are looking more closely at corporate environmental costs and potential environmental liabilities and how these may affect share performance. What is emerging is an understanding that corporations that treat the environment badly will eventually treat their investors badly. Investors will not take kindly to losses resulting from corporate environmental insensitivity or carelessness.

Anecdotal, if not empirical, evidence suggests a growing concern on the part of managers and executives worldwide over environmental issues, with particular interest in moving toward more sustainable business practices. One prime example is the keynote address titled "The Eco-Odyssey of a CEO" delivered at the U.S. Green Building Conference in August 1995 by Ray C. Anderson, chair and CEO of Interface, a global manufacturer of carpet tiles. In that presentation, Anderson noted,

> For 21 of our 22 years of existence, I, for one, never gave one thought to what we were taking from the earth or doing to the earth, except to be sure that we were in compliance and keeping ourselves clean in a regulatory sense... until one year ago... We organized a task force with representatives from all of our businesses from around the world to review Interface's worldwide environmental position. Through pure serendipity, someone sent me a book, Paul Hawken's *The Ecology of Commerce: A Declaration of Sustainability*. This book changed my life. It provided me with a vision and a very powerful sense of urgency.
>
> I offered the task force my vision to make Interface the first name in industrial ecology, worldwide, through substance, not words. I also gave them a mission: to convert Interface into a restorative enterprise, first to reach sustainability, and then to become restorative—putting back more than we ourselves take from the earth.
>
> We coined a word, PLETSUS, standing for Practices LEading Toward SUStainability. We have devised what we believe to be the world's first perpetual lease for carpet tiles, something we call Evergreen Lease. We don't just manufacture the carpet, we install and maintain it. We selectively replace worn and damaged areas, one 18-inch square at a time... In other words, we continue to own the carpet and have the ultimate liability for used carpet tiles. Of course, the economic viability for us depends on our closing the loop, i.e., being able to recycle the used face fiber into new face fiber, and used carpet tile backing into new carpet tile backing. We aren't there yet, but we will get there—becoming sustainable by converting our linear processes into cyclical processes so that we never have to take another drop of oil from the earth. Our vision is zero scrap going to the landfill and zero emissions going to the ecosystem.

## CONCLUSION

So, how should analysts and investors assess the quality of earnings in the years ahead? A sound analytical framework should include the following perspectives:

- Begin with a thorough understanding of the nature of the business, its markets, and its customers.

- Rank the degree of difficulty in determining the company's periodic revenues and expenses and in periodically identifying and measuring its assets and liabilities. Such a ranking should go from "very straightforward" at one extreme to "very subjective" at the other.

- For businesses ranked as straightforward, compare their selection of accounting methods and estimates with others within the industry. Where significant differences are found, proceed with caution and make sure that management's explanations are reasonable and substantive.

- For businesses ranked as subjective, understand the limits of the historical financial statements right from the beginning. Identify the significant revenues and/or expenses most subject to misstatement, and determine the effects of any such misstatements on the balance sheet. In addition, consider the extent to which these businesses might have significant assets or liabilities that are difficult to identify and/or measure in accordance with current accounting standards. Look for significant differences from industry practices with respect to accounting methods and/or estimates.

- The more subjective the accounting and reporting process becomes, the greater the likelihood that the nature of the business is somewhat outside the scope of current accounting standards in terms of capturing reality in a timely fashion. Here is where an honest assessment of the business itself, of management's accounting and reporting practices, and of management's competence and integrity becomes critically important. Here, unfortunately, is also where the lure of "hitting the jackpot" can sometimes overcome good judgment and lead to unfortunate decisions.

- Finally, go back to the beginning and rethink the business fundamentals and the quality of management one last time.

# Question and Answer Session

E. Richard Brownlee II

**Question:** What are your thoughts on the presentation of cash earnings per share versus the usual presentation of generally accepted accounting principles?

**Brownlee:** One of the dilemmas in practice and one of the debates in academia between the accounting and finance people is the role of accrual earnings as a predictor of future cash flows. Given that valuation models are generally cash flow driven, do other measures do a better job of predicting future cash flows? The usefulness of a cash flow per share approach rests on the measure of cash flow. For instance, if we could agree on a cash flow from operations measure and a standard earnings per share calculation, then the two could be combined in a logical cash flow per share measure. Reporting and interpretation problems notwithstanding, cash flow is critically important, and I would encourage creative experimentation for its measurement within our existing reporting model.

**Question:** How can shareholder advisory councils be helpful in improving business reporting?

**Brownlee:** These councils can be an important tool in response to the need to look at forward-looking information and as part of a comprehensive investor communications program. The financial statements can only do so much. The need for future information will be met by ascertaining what management is thinking, what its strategies are and its credibility—the good with the bad.

**Question:** Many companies are now preceding their earnings reports with a long description of their observations for the future. How does legal vulnerability affect willingness and ability of companies to communicate verbally to the shareholders?

**Brownlee:** This so-called "legal problem" is not a big deal for many people around the world, which is why they can and do experiment in financial reporting much more than we do in the United States. People worldwide have trouble understanding how we in the United States have trapped ourselves.

The SEC is trying to provide safe harbor requirements/options to provide more flexibility. In addition, the judicial development known as the "bespeaks caution" doctrine should facilitate additional disclosures of forward-looking information.

**Question:** How useful is the management discussion and analysis (MD&A) section of a financial report?

**Brownlee:** Accounting exists because it tries to portray the essential aspects of the business. We really want to understand what is happening in the business. Where is it going? Where are its markets? Where are its customers? What is changing? What is management thinking? What is its strategy? How does it measure performance? The MD&A can be extremely useful; what is needed are ways of encouraging and improving the whole MD&A concept, including segment reporting and externalizing management's view of the business—both positive and negative.

Well-done MD&As could supplement and even be more useful than, say, *pro forma* financial reports. They would also reinforce what I perceive to be an encouraging trend, that of top management dealing with the investment community in a much more open, honest manner than previously. We will see more and more evidence, such as MD&As, of companies wanting to be perceived as dealing openly and fairly with the investment community. The market will ultimately penalize those companies that behave otherwise.

**Question:** Please comment on economic value added (EVA®) and return on invested capital.

**Brownlee:** These are good attempts at expanding the view of a company's economic reality. We must still have a measure of earnings, however; the problem remains of how we measure financial performance from the earnings perspective. EVA simply adds the investment perspective and explores whether we are earning enough, given the investment we have. We still have to deal with the earnings measure. Many companies, Coca-Cola for example, look at operating earnings, in which case we are back to familiar issues: When is a sale a sale, when should expenses be recorded, do we have an earnings figure that captures economic reality, what is the effect of soft assets?

**Question:** How should companies report environmental expenses?

**Brownlee:** In the next few years, we will see accounting treatment similar to that for pensions and health care, and a liability, often a very large one, will appear where none existed before. More focus will be placed on environment contingencies and the resulting financial liabilities. Look outside the United States to see the shape of trends in this area; much of the leadership is coming from Europe. Such organizations as The Natural Step, based in Stockholm, are taking a leadership role in helping businesses around the world develop a framework for understanding environmental issues based on scientific consensus. Of course, the real key to environmental concern rests at the front end. The real breakthrough will come when businesses routinely include sustainability considerations in their product designs.

# The Subtleties of Reporting Earnings

Martin S. Fridson, CFA
*Chief High-Yield Strategist*
*Merrill Lynch*

> The view that financial reporting is a way to obtain cheap capital provides a fresh context for evaluating reported earnings. The reporting process involves many subtleties, such as information asymmetry, timing, and earnings management, which if not explicit and acceptable, can at least be made understandable.

What is the purpose of financial reporting? The answer is simple—to obtain cheap capital.[1] And if that simple answer is correct, then some purposes to which many analysts and investors subscribe do not hold. For instance, the purpose of financial reports is not to hold up a mirror to a company to let the world know how the company is doing. More importantly, the purpose is not, as the Financial Accounting Standards Board (FASB) suggests, to provide financial information that is useful for making investment decisions. For corporations to adopt such an altruistic purpose would be very surprising; indeed, if they did, they probably would not be serving their shareholders better than they do by seeking to obtain cheap capital in the stock and bond markets.

Seen against this backdrop, the subtleties of reporting earnings become, if not explicit and acceptable, at least understandable. My presentation examines several of those earnings subtleties, drawing on such diverse but related topics as market efficiency, cash flow, reporting assumptions, timing, earnings management, and traditional financial analysis.

## MARKET EFFICIENCY AND INFORMATION ASYMMETRY

Traditional views of market efficiency and information asymmetry may require rethinking if the purpose of financial reporting is to obtain cheap capital. For instance, a fundamental notion in the academic literature in finance states that one way to minimize the cost of capital is to minimize asymmetry of information. The thinking is this: If a corporation has information that investors lack, investors will assign an uncertainty premium to the corporation's expected earnings. If the corporation then shares that information, thereby reducing the disparity in information, it can eliminate the unnecessary and costly uncertainty premium.

This idea is not completely preposterous. One piece of evidence to support minimizing asymmetry of information is the fact that many corporations published financial statements voluntarily before that disclosure became mandatory under securities legislation enacted in the 1930s. Even today, some disclosures regularly seen in quarterly and annual reports are not mandatory. Evidently, some companies believe that reducing the gap between what they know and what investors know reduces their cost of capital.

Reducing information asymmetry, however, is not the only option. An argument can be made for preserving information asymmetry. Suppose a pharmaceutical manufacturer discloses that it has a miraculous new drug in development, a product with the potential to increase corporate earnings spectacularly. The company's stock rises sharply on this disclosure. At that point, the company makes an offer to acquire, using its stock as payment, another pharmaceutical manufacturer. After the acquisition is completed, the company gradually releases the full story about its promising drug, which is not progressing through the process of U.S. Food and Drug Administration approval as easily as the market had expected. The company's stock price plummets, but in the meantime, the company has managed to buy a large chunk of earnings through an acquisition that it made with temporarily inflated currency—its own common stock. The currency was inflated because it

---

[1] Fernando Alvarez of Rutgers University has succinctly summarized the purpose of financial reporting in this manner in his classroom lectures.

Copyright © 1996 Merrill Lynch, Pierce, Fenner & Smith Incorporated.

exploited a gap between what the company knew about the drug's prospects and what the market knew. Clearly, this company would not have been better off minimizing information asymmetry.

A typical criticism of maintaining asymmetry is this one: What about reputational capital? If a company deceives investors by financial reporting trickery, investors will penalize that company in the future because they no longer trust it. Is this reaction observed in the real world? *Barron's* reports from time to time on companies going public that are managed or at least controlled by convicted felons. These characters embezzle or swindle shareholders, which presumably reduces the companies' reputational capital. Yet, they manage to raise investment capital again and again, often on favorable terms.

The "fly-by-night operators" are not the only ones who survive losses of credibility. The book *Financial Warnings* contains many cases of negative earnings surprises that have occurred during the past several years.[2] A common thread is discretionary choices in financial reporting that have created or may in the future create an unpleasant shock to the market. Among the companies included are such blue chips as General Motors Corporation, the Procter & Gamble Company, and IBM Corporation. A recent example is the Coca-Cola Company, which has done an excellent job as measured by economic value added (EVA®) but which in the third quarter of 1996 had a $200 million negative earnings surprise associated with loading up, or what the *New York Times* called "stuffing," its distribution channels.

Are these companies corporate pariahs? Hardly. Their P/E multiples might be higher if their financial reporting were more transparent, but until and unless analysts learn to discriminate between solid earnings and earnings of very dubious quality, companies may be correct in saying, "Forget reputational capital. We are better off maximizing information asymmetry than trying to reduce it." Furthermore, a company's CEO may gain more in present value by boosting reported earnings, thereby raising the current bonus, than will be lost in the stock's value when the problem comes to light—after the CEO has retired.

So, how can analysts and investors identify those companies that desire informational asymmetry, that apparently believe their reputational capital is not at risk? An important first step is to understand some of the subtleties of reporting earnings, especially those that may work, at least in the short run, to reduce the cost of capital.

---

[2]Eugene Comiskey and Charles Mulford (New York: John Wiley & Sons, 1996).

## THE CASH SHUTTLE

A commonly accepted notion among academicians is that the market understands the difference between earnings and cash flow; if a company uses a financial reporting technique that overstates earnings, but does so in a way that is fairly obvious, that fact is not reflected in the market's assessment of the company's cash flow. Much research has been done on events that affect earnings but not cash flow. The conclusion tends to be that the market does not react to such events, that it is sophisticated enough to understand the difference. Anecdotal evidence and the lessons of history, however, say just the opposite.

*Bloomberg Business News*, on October 17, 1996, stated that the accounting authorities in the United Kingdom had relaxed their position on a proposal to require pubs to depreciate their fixed assets over time. Pub owners had rebelled against the idea of having to write off such assets over time. The proposed accounting changes had nothing to do with cash flow, taxes, earnings, or anything else except reported earnings. What's more, analysts could, if they so desired, deduct the value of fixed assets for themselves by deducting a percentage of the value of plant and equipment every year. *Bloomberg* reported that the pubs' stock prices rose when the U.K. Accounting Standards Board softened its stance. Analysts were quoted as saying this backdown on financial reporting changes was good news. They spoke about which companies' earnings would have been hurt the most by the previously proposed rules. This incident as reported seems to fly in the face of the notion that the market understands the difference between cash flow and earnings.

### The Savings and Loan Strategy

If I give you a dollar and you hand it right back to me, neither of us has enjoyed an increase in wealth, but the accounting rules disagree with that conclusion. The accounting standards say that shuffling money back and forth generates earnings, which means wealth is created. Consider the case of a savings and loan (S&L) that finances a developer even though few good projects are available at the time. The developer says, "If I can borrow some money on speculation, things may turn around; by the time I get the project built, some tenants may be out there." In the meantime, though, the project and the tenants are only wishful thinking.

So, where is the developer going to get the money to pay the interest? Out of the money the S&L just loaned. When that dollar comes back into the S&L, the accountants call it revenue, which produces income. This project could be completely uneconomical and completely nonviable. It could have no prospect of creating wealth, but when that money comes back to the S&L, it is called income and added to the reserves so that more loans can be created. Overlending to cover interest expense is a common means of generating paper profits, as well as regulatory capital to support more loans.

S&Ls in the 1980s took this strategy to great and sophisticated lengths. Basically, the S&L lends to the developer, and the interest comes back in, which produces an accounting profit. One of the effects is that the CEO receives a portion of this profit in the form of a performance-based bonus. So, the CEO has an incentive to lend more and more on the same economically nonviable basis because that means more and more reported earnings. The developer is getting some money out of this transaction also and if no promising projects are around, can at least receive a salary for a few years. Also, because the loan-to-value ratio is at least 100 percent, the developer, having no equity in the project, does not care if it fails and may well walk away and wait until conditions get better.

How much equity does the CEO or the group controlling the S&L have in the project? In the early 1980s, when a lot of S&Ls were already failing, the U.S. Federal Deposit Insurance Corporation required controlling groups, in theory, to put down 5 percent of the assets, but of course, no one wanted to do that. So the group simply created some fictitious equity and effectively acquired the institution while putting down no cash. When the deal inevitably failed, the S&L managers walked away, unless the government could prove fraud, which was not easy.

To avoid being taken in, the analyst's basic task was, and is, to determine whether genuinely economically viable projects can succeed in the environment at the time. The vacancy rate is probably the best single indicator, but the nature of the sample of properties is crucial: Are there different types of properties that might have different vacancy rates? Also, the investigation should go beyond the financial statements. Analysts need to go to the area where the developer operates, walk around, and see how many buildings are leased, how many malls have empty stores in them, whether an office building has many vacancies, and what sort of incentives are being offered to prospective tenants.

## The Advanced S&L Strategy: A Ponzi Scheme

S&Ls also needed money to lend in the 1980s. So, they advertised jumbo certificates of deposit at very high interest rates and attracted depositors from all over the country. Where did they get the money to pay the depositors' interest? They brought in new depositors at an even higher CD rate and took some of that money to pay off the interest to the first group.

This tactic was nothing but a Ponzi scheme. In the 1920s, Charles Ponzi used a basic ingenious scam that has been replicated many times in many countries: Promise very high rates of return; bring in new investors; take their money; and provide those high returns to the initial investors, which encourages even more investors. Eventually, the scheme has to collapse, and for the S&Ls that operated this way, it did.

All of the S&Ls' new income was reported as earnings, but the reality was just a shuttling of cash in order to report earnings. All of this activity created no economic value, but under the accounting rules, all those deposits turned into income. Of course, at the end of this Ponzi chain was the deposit insurance fund, or more specifically, U.S. taxpayers. Clearly, the moral is that analysts have to look behind the enterprise. Perhaps another moral is that accounting should be taught as part of a broader business education, because the numbers on the income statements may not, often do not, provide a picture of business reality.

## The Franchise Strategy

No one disputes that the restaurant business is a very tough way to make profits. Many people in that business undervalue their own labor to sell their product at a price that is too low for anyone to make a profit. So, restaurants would seem to be a poor business to go into, much less to try to take public. A typical strategy has been to generate sales growth at a very high rate; earnings are another matter. Eventually, the enterprise is supposed to make a profit, but in the meantime, if an owner keeps adding restaurants to the chain, a very small base can produce a tremendous rate of growth in sales. On the strength of that performance, the owner takes the business public, sells a lot of stock, and gets as much cash out of the deal as quickly as possible before the business fails. The operation shows a lot of growth but no profits.

People have now come up with a more sophisticated approach. They have finally conceded that being in the restaurant business is not attractive, but being in the restaurant *franchising* business can be very attractive. They sell franchises to fee-paying operators. The fee is for advertising, the "concept," the recipes, the promotion, educational support, and all the rest. The franchise seller itself is not in the restaurant business. It just collects fees.

A problem arises if the franchisees are not profitable, however. They are selling sandwiches, but they are not making money. Where are they going to get the money to pay the fees? The parent company simply goes to Wall Street, raises some money in the stock market, and distributes it among the franchise operators, who turn around and give the money right back.

According to the accountants, the money that the franchise seller receives represents revenues, from which a profit derives. The public company has earnings, on the strength of which it can go out and sell more stock and create more franchises. So, the franchise seller can stay in business for quite a while without ever making a real economic profit. If the controlling shareholders are fortunate enough to be able to sell some of their stock before the business unwinds, they can earn handsome returns even though the enterprise fails. As long as the equity market continues to pay for the false earnings, franchise holders' losses can be transformed into public company profits.

## THE POWER OF ASSUMPTIONS

Underlying assumptions probably lead to more earnings distortions than any other single factor. Both companies and investors can do amazing things with assumptions; common examples include the use of leverage, the recognition of a sale, and the treatment of depreciation, development costs, and loss reserves.

### Making Leverage Work

The most dramatic example in recent years of the power of assumptions has been in transactions that might be called overleveraged buyouts. Some LBOs worked out well in the early 1980s, but by the mid- to late 1980s, everybody seemed to be doing LBOs, especially small and medium-sized LBOs, for which there supposedly was not a lot of competition. But a lot of money was chasing a limited number of deals, so a good idea became overdone.

A lot of assumptions were common as the deals progressed—for instance, that the LBO would be financed by selling off all of the assets at a higher multiple than was just paid. Another common assumption was that a mature, commodity-oriented company could, through the power of leverage exerted on management, take 300 basis points out of its operating expenses—in a business that was highly competitive and already relatively "lean." The further assumption was that cutting highly visible (but relatively immaterial) operating expenses, such as a corporate jet or hunting lodge, in the near term could make the earnings look great. Research studies compounded the illusion by indicating that LBOs were tremendously successful; unfortunately, many of these studies were done only a short time after the LBOs were completed. The longer term impact of cutbacks in advertising and research could not be evaluated. (In one notorious case, a study sample included LBOs that had not yet been completed. The authors merely assumed in their measures of LBO "success" that operating margins would improve.)

### When Is a Sale a Sale?

When should a sale be recognized? It is a question of certainty. A common answer to the question is that when a company performs a service, the sale should be recognized within the context of a reasonable provision for possible failure to collect debts. Nonetheless, levels of confidence about performing the service, and thus points of recognition, vary. Even within an individual industry, the practice of revenue recognition varies tremendously. For example, a sale might be recognized when the product is shipped to a customer, when the customer receives the product, when the product is actually installed, when the product undergoes final testing, or when the customer makes final payment for the product. Different companies might use any of these events as the point of recognizing revenues. In general, the sale is more certain the closer the customer is to the revenue recognition; that is, recognition at the point of customer payment is certainly a more conservative stance than recognition at shipment to the customer.

Software companies present a prime example of the revenue-recognition problem. Software is an ongoing business and clearly different from R&D in the traditional sense. The companies are producing and selling the product at the same time they are developing it. The financial statements provide very limited help, so analysts have to look at the business itself and ultimately the product. The company may be doing lots of work, enabling it to recognize more and more revenue, without coming any closer to producing a viable product. If the project ultimately fails, the basis for revenue recognized up to that point will be compromised.

### Stretching Depreciable Life

Assumptions about depreciation are also very important. Most companies have to show some wear and tear on the equipment. This practice may well be part of a mental reserve in the minds of management: When earnings go down, management will suddenly decide that the depreciable lives of the assets ought to be longer than before; magically, the earnings loss will be offset by a gain that has nothing to do with anything economic. **Table 1** shows the effects on earnings of extending depreciable life of property, plant, and equipment (PP&E) by just one year. After the accounting change, net income increases by $600,000 with no changes in any real economic input. The decision as to the "right" depreciable life is not an objective one. These sorts of decisions involve

**Table 1. Effect of Depreciable Life Extension on the Income Statement**
($ millions)

| Item | Eight-Year Depreciable Life of PP&E | Nine-Year Depreciable Life of PP&E |
|---|---|---|
| Sales | $100.0 | $100.0 |
| Product costs | 70.0 | 70.0 |
| Depreciation | 8.8 | 7.8 |
| Interest | $ 2.0 | $ 2.0 |
| Pretax income | 19.2 | 20.2 |
| Income tax | 6.5 | 6.9 |
| Net income | $ 12.7 | $ 13.3 |

*Source*: Martin S. Fridson.

much discretion, and the timing of changes tends to be rather curious.

A few years ago, several steel mills changed to a unit-of-production depreciation method. It had been used in the mining industry, which is a fairly low-technology industry. A mine would shut down for a couple of years at a time because ore prices were low, and equipment usage was not continuous. So, it made sense to try to gauge the actual physical wear and tear on the equipment, to determine (after so many units of production) that the equipment was now used up, and make that determination the basis for the depreciation schedule. The case for the steel mills using that method is weaker than for the coal mines. Like the mines, the mills have shutdowns and physical wear and tear, but the mills are more technologically dynamic, so the justification for halting the depreciation clock while the plant is shut down for six months or a year is not clear. Although the physical wear and tear ceases, deterioration in value may continue as the mills become increasingly outdated in their technology. Of course, once one steel company adopted the unit-of-production method, then the others followed suit to conform to "standard industry practice," which is almost invariably a liberalization.

## New Industries and Development Costs

New industries typically use their accounting discretion liberally. It takes a while for the accountants—even legitimately, with the best of intentions—to come up with what the standards ought to be. In a subscription-type operation, for instance, no one knows what the customer turnover will be; in a leasing business, no one knows what the recoveries on leased equipment will be. The treatment of development costs is a particularly pervasive issue.

Several years ago, a waste disposal company claimed it had, and was perceived by Wall Street as having, a conservative accounting system. The company, however, was capitalizing much of the indirect development costs of obtaining and developing land sites. Most people agree that some of that cost should be capitalized, but such expenses as entertaining municipal officials are not clearly capital costs. As it turned out, the amount of capitalization in question was the difference between that company's earnings and the earnings of its competitors that were bidding on the same contracts and incurring the same kinds of expenses. For a company to have a substantially larger profit margin than companies in the exact same business certainly raises questions. Such a company will always have a story about how it has better managers, but analysts should always ask for something more specific as to how the company is able to achieve much larger profit margins than comparable companies. Miraculous things happen to earnings with the use of liberal assumptions about recoveries in such areas as indirect development costs and interest.

## Loss Reserves

Another facet of earnings that is prone to assumptions is the question of expected losses. Finance companies, for example, have a range of potential borrowers—some good-quality credits, some risky ones. Most of the credits are going to be somewhere in the middle of the distribution. Suppose a financial services company establishes its credit cutoff right in the middle of the curve, categorizing anything below that point as the lowest quality of credit. The result of applying that standard is shown in **Table 2**. Column 2 shows the company's Year 1 income statement with a reserve for losses. The losses actually incurred are from loans generated in earlier periods, but the company is recognizing current revenues and a reasonable set-aside for loss.

To raise earnings during a flat period in the economy, assume that management suddenly shifts the credit standard downward in order to make more loans. In the financial services business, revenues are easy to raise: Lower the credit standards, increase the revenues. The result, given in the Year 2 income statement (third column), is a much-improved top line, virtually unchanged fixed costs, and a handsome earnings increase for the year.

The only snag is that management, not commensurately raising its assumption about expected losses,

### Table 2. Effect of Lowering Standards on Reported Earnings
($ millions except as noted)

| Item | Mean Year 1 Credit Quality | Lower Year 2 Credit Quality |
|---|---|---|
| Finance charges | $100 | $110 |
| Other income | 15 | 15 |
| Total revenue | $115 | $125 |
| Interest expense | 47 | 52 |
| Fixed costs | 35 | 35 |
| Loss reserve at 15% | 15 | 17 |
| Pretax income | $ 18 | $ 21 |
| Tax at 35% | 6 | 7 |
| Net income | $ 12 | $ 14 |
| Shares outstanding (number, based on equity required to support loan portfolio) | 10 | 11 |
| Earnings per share | $1.20 | $1.27 |

*Source*: Martin S. Fridson.

still reserves only 15 percent. Proper adjustment of the reserve to reflect the lower-quality credit risks accepted would cause the increase in earnings to disappear, as will inevitably occur anyway. Eventually, actual realized losses will vary adversely from the picture now being presented by management. The company will have a write-off, which will be explained away but undoubtedly not by reference to the excessively liberal loss reserve assumptions in earlier periods.

Analysts must look at the quality of earnings and any earnings increase. Does the pattern reflect what is going on among competitors? If others are showing flat or deteriorating earnings in the same environment, what is so special about this company that enables it to continue to show earnings growth in a period such as this one?

## TIMING IS EVERYTHING

Reported earnings reflect timing considerations of various types ranging from the general seasonality of earnings to such specific issues as bridge loans, derivatives, and earnings advances.

### The Seasonality of Earnings

Table 3 shows an example of differences in quarterly earnings figures by comparing two companies. Retailer A and Retailer B, like many retailers, receive the bulk of their earnings in the fourth quarter, around the Christmas season. In Year 1, Retailer A consistently earned $20 million for the first three quarters and then made $60 million in the fourth quarter. That increase is not an improvement in any sense, because the bulk of its earnings is expected to come in the fourth quarter. Given the seasonality of this business, the quarter-to-quarter progression is less important than what the fourth quarter should be relative to the same quarter in the previous year. In Year 2, the company has a 10 percent increase in earnings over Year 1 in the first through third quarters, but the fourth quarter is down 10 percent from the preceding year. Because earnings are down, the stock price goes down, which is bad news for the company.

Retailer B is a clone of Retailer A in that its budget is exactly the same: $20 million a quarter for three quarters and then $60 million in the fourth. In Year 1,

### Table 3. Seasonality of Earnings: Examples of Quarterly Earnings Progression: Budget versus Actual
($ millions except as noted)

| Example | 1Q | 2Q | 3Q | 4Q |
|---|---|---|---|---|
| *Retailer A* | | | | |
| Year 1 budget | $20 | $20 | $20 | $60 |
| Year 1 actual | 20 | 20 | 20 | 60 |
| Year 2 actual | 22 | 22 | 22 | 54 |
| Year-over-year change | +10% | +10% | +10% | –10% |
| *Retailer B* | | | | |
| Year 1 budget | $20 | $20 | $20 | $60 |
| Year 1 actual | 20 | 18 | 16 | 40 |
| Year 2 actual | 10 | 11 | 13 | 36 |
| Year-over-year change | –50% | –39% | –19% | –10% |

*Source*: Martin S. Fridson.

B started off on budget but then began to slip. Actual earnings were $18 million in the second quarter, 10 percent below budget; $16 million in the third quarter, 20 percent below budget; and $40 million in the fourth quarter, 33 percent below budget. The fact that the company is doing poorly relative to budget is clearly going to be perceived as negative.

Moreover, the company continued to deteriorate. In the first quarter of Year 2, it earned $10 million, down by fully 50 percent in a year-over-year comparison. At this point, Retailer B's management began to take decisive action. Earnings were down by only 39 percent on a year-over-year basis in the second quarter and only 19 percent year over year in the third quarter. In the fourth quarter of the year, earnings were up from the third quarter, as usual, but down 10 percent from the fourth quarter a year ago.

Is it time to sell the stock of Retailer B in light of the year-over-year earnings decrease? Or is it time to buy the stock in light of the fourth-quarter earnings report? Or is more information needed? An analyst might well regard the management actions that caused the earnings decline to decelerate as good news. But many, perhaps most, investors look at the earnings only on a year-over-year basis because of their seasonality. High-yield bond investors, for instance, reacting reflexively to a year-over-year decline, would tend to view the fourth-quarter report as bad news. A look at the larger picture, especially the earnings progression, persuades me that they are misinterpreting the facts.

## Bridge Loans

Discussing bridge loans takes us back once more to the LBO era. Suppose an investment bank saw a deal with the potential for substantial merger and acquisition (M&A) fees. To compete for that business, it backed one of the bidders in what turned out to be a bidding war for the property. The bidders were then in a good position, playing one investment bank against another. Clearly, the idea was to transfer the risk of the transaction from the bidders to someone else, the investment banks, if possible.

The idea of the bridge loan evolved from this type of transaction, which was done on the investment bank's own balance sheet and came to be known as checkbook financing. The investment bank says, "We are going to back you with the understanding that if you win, you will do your underwriting business with us. Of course, we are not going to consider those fees when we make this loan. The loan is going to be completely freestanding, justified on its own merits without any thought of the $50 million in fees that we are going to earn if our candidate wins." This attitude involves a lot of self-delusion, because the likelihood is that the loan will, in effect, be generously subsidized and does not have merit on a stand-alone basis.

So, in the first year, the bank makes the bridge loan to the bidder and books the M&A and underwriting fees. The fees are earned up front, but the loss on the bridge loan may take a while; it occurs when the deal starts to unravel because it was not financed adequately. Assume the bridge loan loss occurs in the second year; the bank may well give the borrower some forbearance: "I know you are short this quarter, so pay us next quarter." By the third year, the auditors, the accountants, and the risk-management people say that the loan is now genuinely bad, that the bank must recognize the loss. In effect, the bank has bought current profits with future losses.

Clearly, a financial services company can buy a lot of business by lowering its standards and subsidizing bidders. It can book a lot of revenues, so-called profits, which are really the illusion of profits because those revenues will be given back by the losses on the bridge loans plus problems arising on the underwritings and expenses connected with the loan.

A key issue in the whole bridge loan affair is: When does the investment banker who puts this deal together receive the requisite bonus. Of course, it is at the inception of the transaction, which fueled the fervor to do such deals.

One piece of good news is that some positive reforms are occurring on this front, based on the model of the venture capital business. The norm in the venture capital industry is for deal makers to get paid for deals over a period of several years. The venture capital firms wait to see if the transaction has made money before they lavish out rewards. Some businesses may not be able to use such a long period because of competition in the labor markets, but that approach is the right kind of system. Making the timing of the economic profits being earned correspond with the bonuses being paid out is a positive change.

## Derivatives

The financial reporting problem in derivatives is accounting for risk, which like the bridge loan difficulty, turns out to be a timing problem. Derivatives do not eliminate risk; rather, they redistribute it. One way to redistribute risk is to concentrate it all in one short period of time, which may be in the future. In a lot of derivatives transactions, profits can be leveraged up dramatically in the near term. Again, a company can reward the people involved in the current period based on those profits, even though they inevitably will be offset by a loss at a later point. The reason is that the risk that justified those returns has not been eliminated; it has merely been shifted forward.

Some financial services businesses, which tend to be very competitive, earn extraordinary profits this way, and the investment management business is no exception. In short-term money market or intermediate bond funds, for instance, the group return might be very tightly concentrated around 8 percent but some managers are making 12 percent. They do it by shifting a lot of risk to a future period. They make great returns now but inevitably will give it all back later.

## Earnings Advances

A very clever timing device relating to earnings advances came to light recently. A non-U.S. home-building supplies retailer was able to boost its earnings by prematurely recognizing volume discounts offered by its suppliers. If the company buys a certain amount of lumber over a period of time, it receives a volume discount, but it does not earn the discount until it has bought that volume of lumber. Management appears to have been recognizing in the current period the volume discounts that it expected to earn in future periods. The risk, of course, was that the company would never earn those discounts. A new CEO brought into the retailer, unaware of prior management practices, launched an investigation when the company suddenly had an increase in revenues but the profits did not rise commensurately. Of course, he found that the company had been, by necessity, making up for its previous borrowing of future earnings. It was impossible for future profits to rise in concert with sales increases because the volume discounts on those new sales had already been recognized.

## EARNINGS MANAGEMENT TECHNIQUES

Analysts must be vigilant for an almost limitless variety of earnings management techniques; the following examples give an idea of the creativity and distortion that can be involved.

- Inventory valuation. A retailer may switch to a company-specific price index for valuing LIFO inventories.
- Current revenue. A broadcaster, failing to sell all commercial time, runs extra spots for its major advertisers and recognizes current revenue.
- Production costs. A film studio, assuming high sales in video and airline exhibition, leaves the production costs of a "flop" in a capitalized state.
- Payment periods. A computer manufacturer props up revenues by stretching out payment periods, offering partial refunds in the event of future price reductions, and allowing customers to try the equipment without making an initial payment.
- Depreciable lives. A producer of security equipment lengthens depreciable lives of rental equipment, which causes certain leases to be reclassified from sales to operating, thereby increasing net income.

Two of these cases merit more detailed examination. With regard to the film studio's production costs, previously published research by John Tinker showed that Orion Pictures would inevitably have a write-off because it aggressively capitalized the production costs of films based on assumptions about future revenues—specifically, that the airline and video markets would somehow be lucrative even though no one had wanted to see the movie in theaters.[3] What Tinker showed was that the company's capitalized production costs were rising steadily relative to sales. The revenues were basically flat, but the capitalized production costs were going up. Compared with the industry norm, a gap existed that would result in a write-off. In about a year, Orion took the write-off, exactly as Tinker had predicted. A couple of years later, Orion repeated the same process, and newspaper headlines reported that the market was shocked by earnings surprises at Orion Pictures. Why? It had happened before, but this time it seemed to be totally unexpected.

With regard to the security equipment's depreciable life, ordinarily, the way to liberalize earnings is to extend the depreciable lives of assets, but the approach can be a bit quirky. For a company that leased security equipment, the quirk turned out to be that the difference between operating leases and capital leases depended, in part, on the length of the life of the equipment that was being leased. When the company assumed a shorter depreciable life on rental equipment, it switched its accounting method, causing certain leases to be reclassified from sales-type leases to operating leases and improving its reported earnings. So, what looked like a conservative change in the company's accounting system actually liberalized its reported earnings.

Analysts must also be aware that one company may be practicing many earnings management techniques, with an almost bewildering variety of earnings effects. An article published in 1994 cited a company whose financial reporting was fairly well disclosed; that is, the footnotes permitted observers to piece together what was happening, although not necessarily the magnitude in each quarter.[4] The company was not at all apologetic about using the following earnings

---

[3]*Financial Statement Analysis: A Practitioner's Guide* (New York: John Wiley & Sons, 1991).

management techniques: (1) changing accounting treatment of postretirement benefits, (2) using restructuring charges to offset gains on asset sales, (3) manipulating the timing of sales of equity kickers and warrants obtained in lending, (4) manipulating the timing of acquisitions to "buy earnings," (5) delaying write-offs, and (6) allocating goodwill in acquisitions disproportionately to the portions that were not to be sold.

One might attribute this behavior to a corporate "can do" mentality in which trickery, but not failure, is tolerated. Does it work? The company perennially ranks very high on EVA and does an excellent job of creating shareholder value. Its management is lionized regularly in the financial press. The stock market is avidly buying its shares. Its success may be a combination of good legitimate management and some gimmicks, but the gimmicks are not depleting the company's reputational capital. The company appears to show no inclination to reduce this informational asymmetry. If the purpose of financial reporting is to raise cheap capital, this company's methods seem to work.

## DETECTION IS POSSIBLE

For anyone who may think that this picture is too bleak and that there is no hope at all, one recently

[4]Randall Smith, Steven Lipin, and Amal Kumar Naj, "Managing Profits: How General Electric Dumps Fluctuations in Its Corporate Earnings," *Wall Street Journal* (November 3, 1994):A1, A6.

published example showed that some of these problems are detectable. The basic idea of looking at financial ratios is extremely powerful. The failure of events to move in a logical way—evidenced by one income statement item out of line with another or by a balance sheet item out of line with an income statement number—often can be what gives away the earnings game. Ratios can indeed enable analysts to detect earnings problems from the outside and challenge management on those problems.

In the late 1980s, MiniScribe Corporation, a manufacturer of computer disk drives, was recording fictitious sales as revenues. Eventually, this practice came to light, and the market at that point adjusted the firm's stock price downward. Earlier red flags were certainly there, however, for those who looked. **Figure 1** shows three very basic ratios (current liabilities to net worth, collection period, and payables period) for MiniScribe and for a peer group of companies. MiniScribe's liability ratio was increasing out of line with the peer group, with no inherent reason why it would change over time. We can infer that MiniScribe was becoming increasingly debt laden as a result of cash shortfalls. The collection period was rising, likewise not a trend that was seen throughout the industry. Here, the implication was that revenues were declining in quality and therefore becoming less realizable. Finally, MiniScribe's payables period was much longer than, and increased faster than, the peer group, indicating that MiniScribe was using payables

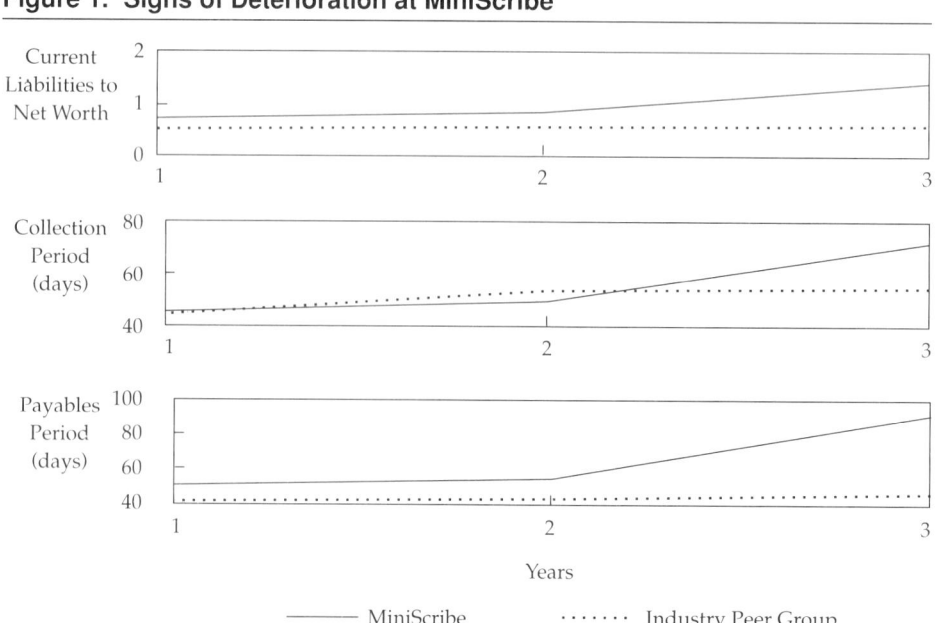

Figure 1. Signs of Deterioration at MiniScribe

*Source*: Philip D. Drake and John W. Peavy III, "Fundamental Analysis, Stock Price, and the Demise of MiniScribe Corporation," *Journal of Portfolio Management* (Spring 1995):68–73.

as a substantial financing source. Again, the underlying problem presumably was inadequate cash flow. Despite MiniScribe's earlier announcements of record earnings (third quarter 1988, for example), all three ratios indicated the illusory nature of those earnings and portended future problems. And in fact, MiniScribe subsequently filed for bankruptcy in 1990.

As suggested by the MiniScribe case, financial gimmicks are probably most frequently detected by the ratios of accounts receivable and inventory to sales. In general, those types of working capital accounts should grow more or less proportionately with sales. Unexpected or involuntary inventory accumulation is perhaps the most common problem that arises, especially in fashion- or technology-oriented businesses, in which the risk of obsolescence is high.

Unlike the MiniScribe example, some financial ratios, assets, earnings, and revenues do not relate in such obvious ways; as suggested in the book *Financial Warnings*, however, these less obvious ratios also can be important. For example, some of the companies that had completely fabricated revenues were able to bury that fact in the fixed plant and equipment accounts in ways that were not apparent to most analysts. One great feature of a double-entry accounting system is that fabricated earnings must have an offset somewhere in the company's accounts, albeit perhaps buried in unexpected places. With today's data-processing technology, calculating every conceivable ratio makes sense. The chances are that if some ratios are getting out of line, something is wrong or not being reported properly.

The practice of calculating ratios is not more widespread largely because the audience for this information is limited mainly to short sellers. Wall Street is criticized because it readily makes buy recommendations but makes few sell recommendations. Yet, some Wall Streeters say that is the way it should be. Sell recommendations, after all, can only go to the people who already own the stock, but buy recommendations can go to everybody. Investors do not have a lot of incentive to find reasons not to buy stocks. The nature of the market is that buy-side analysts are largely on their own in ferreting out potential problems.

## CONCLUSION

Benjamin Graham, the father of securities analysis, told a true story during the 11th annual convention of the National Federation of Financial Analysts Societies, as printed in *The Analysts Journal* in 1958.[5]

[5]"The New Speculation in Common Stocks" (June):17–21.

As a college student, Graham took a semester off to do some work that was very statistical in nature. The company he was involved with had an early model of a machine that used punch cards. This machine, which was produced by a company called Calculating, Tabulating, and Recording, increased the efficiency of bookkeeping and statistical operations dramatically. When Graham got out of school, and took a job as a securities analyst, he told his boss about the great company that made this machine. He said, "I am one of the few people who has used it, because hardly anyone knows about it, but it is really great." Graham's supervisor said, "Forget about it. We have looked at that company, and its balance sheet is water—the assets are phony, there are financial accounting improprieties, and we do not want to go anywhere near that company." For the next 50 years, Graham never owned a single share of this company, which eventually changed its name to IBM.

So, sometimes, an enterprise is actually viable underneath all this maneuvering and shuttling and strategizing. The company may be papering over its problems until it can get going, but if it ultimately is profitable, it can turn into a good investment. In the interim, the company presents a lot of risk on the downside but ultimately some real opportunity on the upside.

Thus, the earnings story is not all black and white. Some investor relations professionals sincerely believe that a corporation's self-interest is to have well-informed shareholders, but that is not the entire picture. Any practicing analyst knows that there is more to the story than enlightened self-interest on the part of corporations. Companies, including respectable blue-chip companies, often find that they can gain more in the short run by maximizing rather than minimizing informational asymmetry.

The point to remember is that companies have a duty to minimize their cost of capital. Successful managers are flexible and pragmatic. That is how they got where they are. If candor works, they will be candid. If playing it close to the vest works, they will probably do that. Money managers and analysts, on the other hand, have a duty to find the best value for their clients. This means that they have to assume that they are not getting all of the relevant information. There is no substitute for hard work and clear-eyed analysis in the attempt to sort out the IBMs from the dubious S&Ls and the restaurant franchises. Investment professionals need to hold companies accountable and to make the term "reputational capital" genuinely mean something, so as to avoid letting those companies get their capital too cheaply.

# Question and Answer Session
## Martin S. Fridson, CFA

**Question:** What questions can you ask management, and what topics do you probe to help you discover more "reality"?

**Fridson:** Comparisons are important. Many companies exhibit isolated events that have no connection to what is happening in the industry. When the ratios are out of line, ask why the effect is not similar for competitors. The companies will tend to emphasize that everybody's product line is a little different. Chemical companies, for example, each have a slightly different mix of chemicals. That comment is valid, but many explanations are not.

Although you need to be skeptical of ratios that do not seem to be in line, you also need to bear down on management when results are unexpectedly good. Ask yourself whether the earnings are somehow being propped up artificially. The emphasis tends to be on the reported earnings expectations, but you tend not to see as much focus on the balance sheet items, which actually offer much useful information. The most important point of all, however, is how credible management has been over time; credibility (or lack of it) builds more credibility (or less of it).

**Question:** Please comment on buying earnings from acquisitions. Who, if anybody, is getting fooled?

**Fridson:** The main way analysts and investors are fooled in general is by depending on electronic data systems, which in this particular case tend to bury a lot of the history of the acquisition. A smooth earnings progression, without all of the underlying detail, creates an unrealistically bullish and possibly deceptive, picture of how steadily the acquiring company has performed. Again, the key is to ask questions. A sudden boost in earnings in a given period for a company that also made an acquisition during that period should cause an analyst to wonder whether the two events are unrelated.

**Question:** Given the sustained bull market of the past three years, who cares about whether financial gimmickry affects investor perception? Shorting the stocks of those "distorted" companies would have been disastrous.

**Fridson:** The question is almost philosophical, one of investment style. Should I go with the momentum and try to anticipate what the other person will do? Or should I assume that on balance, even though I am going to lose sometimes, I will come out ahead if I really hew to a fundamental approach? As a practical matter, can you switch styles back and forth from period to period and be nimble enough always to know which is the right way to go? And from a business standpoint, can you market yourself as an investment manager on that theory, or should you say, "This is the way we approach it, and some markets are going to favor our approach and some are not"? Those are some of the practical realities. If you have a tremendous influx of liquidity into the stock market and everything is going up and no traditional valuation measure holds, then it is certainly valid to ask who cares at the moment. The real question is whether you can throw out all the traditional valuation measures or whether they still count in a broader, longer term context.

**Question:** Please provide the titles of books you consider useful in pointing out these earnings subtleties.

**Fridson:** Mulford and Comiskey's book, *Financial Warnings*, was published by John Wiley & Sons in 1996. Schilit's book, *Financial Shenanigans: How to Detect Accounting Gimmicks and Fraud in Financial Reports*, was published in 1993 by McGraw-Hill. My own book, *Financial Statement Analysis: A Practitioner's Guide*, which is now in its second edition and is published by John Wiley & Sons (1995), partly addresses the reported earnings problem. It is a practitioner's guide and uses examples of what practitioners actually encounter as opposed to what the accounting rules say.

# Searching for Real Earnings: Practical Suggestions

Kathryn F. Staley, CFA
*Gilder, Gagnon, Howe & Company*

> Finding reality in reported earnings is a daunting task in the often frenetic circumstances facing many portfolio managers. That task is made more manageable, however, by focusing on practical interpretation of earnings announcements, key aspects of portfolio maintenance, and useful shortcuts to effective earnings analysis.

Finding reality in reported earnings would be difficult enough in ideal conditions, but it is a daunting task indeed in the circumstances many portfolio managers face—perhaps 200 stocks in a portfolio, maybe 100 more stocks under surveillance, and probably a very small research staff. Research time is always inadequate, and stockholders in today's market seem to be especially adept at recognizing and reacting quickly when economic earnings, particularly if negative, diverge from reported earnings. The typical day is event driven, mostly spent in reaction, with little time for planning or reflection. Taking that "firing line" perspective, this presentation discusses practical interpretation of earnings announcements, offers advice on portfolio maintenance, and suggests useful shortcuts to effective earnings analysis.

## EARNINGS ANNOUNCEMENTS

One way to get ready for the inevitably hectic earnings season is to prepare an earnings calendar. A day of the calendar is filled in with the name of the company, the First Call earnings estimate (I prefer First Call Corporation to Zacks Investment Research or I/B/E/S International simply because First Call estimates seem to be updated more frequently), and the conference call telephone number, if available. This calendar can be backed up by a file containing the last 10-Q, the year-ago 10-Q, the last earnings announcement, and the conference call notes from the previous conference call. These tools provide the background for gleaning earnings insights from income statements, balance sheets, and conference calls.

## Income Statements

The first financial information obtained is typically via an income statement, although it is usually a truncated one without much information. A useful exercise is to take that income statement as it comes across the news wire and determine whether management is delivering what it has promised to deliver. Are the operating prospects as good as anticipated? If not, why not? The following quick checks can help answer those questions:

- Compare stated earnings with the First Call estimate.
- Examine the growth in gross revenues year over year and sequentially through the year.
- Examine gross margins for evidence of any pricing pressures; are the gross margins in line with the previous quarter and the year-ago quarter?
- Determine whether operating margins indicate that selling, general, and administrative (SG&A) expenses are up or down dramatically from the previous quarter.
- Check for the existence and magnitude of other income, although typically that sort of detail is not forthcoming until the conference call or the 10-Q.
- Determine whether a lower tax rate in the quarter added to earnings per share (EPS).

Even this quick analysis will often reveal fads and phases in earnings manipulation; the most popular of these are probably manipulation of depreciation and the allowance for doubtful accounts, addition of nonrecurring revenues, and reduction of SG&A expenses. The following examples illustrate these types of earnings manipulation.

■ *Depreciation.* Foundation Health Corporation released its earnings for the quarter ended September 30, 1996; amortization and depreciation was $9.1 million, down from the year-ago level of $11.3 million and also down from more than $17 million the previous quarter. The reduction in amortization and depreciation contributed about 17 percent of pretax income and added about 10 cents to EPS.

So naturally, a main topic of the conference call was what had changed about depreciation. Did you change the salvage value? Did you change the number of years? Did you sell some assets? Management hemmed and hawed a bit, then said that, after careful study, the company had "reevaluated and conformed the depreciation schedules of certain assets." What assets? The company had determined, again after careful study, that it had overdepreciated computer equipment in the past, and it decided to make the adjustment in the current quarter. Of course, that adjustment allowed the company to match previous earnings estimates exactly. Without the change, it would have been 10 cents short.

A few days later, the company changed its mind, perhaps having been warned by its accountants about being overaggressive, and issued revised results wherein amortization and depreciation expense were increased to $14.5 million for the quarter; the resulting impact on earnings was about 6 cents, still substantial but not quite so blatant as the original case. This is a particularly fruitful example of the earnings effects that can be missed by the harried analyst or portfolio manager who fails to read between the lines.

■ *Allowance for doubtful accounts.* As with depreciation, this figure is not always disclosed in the initial income statement and has to be checked in the balance sheet in the 10-Q by tracking the allowance as a percentage of gross receivables. The best example is a computer game company for hand-held, 16-bit Nintendo games. The company increased the allowance account dramatically in good times and maintained the allowance at very high levels. The word on Wall Street was that when the inevitable change in fads came, the company would then reverse that posture to smooth the EPS in bad quarters. That is exactly what happened: When the fad in games faded, suddenly the allowance for doubtful accounts started getting smaller and smaller as a percentage of gross receivables on the balance sheet. The only problem is that the bad times outlasted the allowance; the allowance was insufficient to continue smoothing EPS, and the stock price plummeted. Watch the trend in the allowance so you will not be surprised when EPS fail to rise.

■ *Nonrecurring revenues.* Also called "other income," nonrecurring revenues can be particularly difficult to find. The management discussion and analysis (MD&A) is usually the most helpful but is no guarantee of accurate presentation. Nearly anyone could have looked at Morrison Knudsen Corporation's income statements for 1991 to 1993 and seen that "other income" was the primary growth vehicle of the company; in 1991, it was almost $36 million of the company's $58 million pretax income, and in 1993, other income and the "gain on sale of subsidiary" totaled nearly 60 percent of pretax income (**Table 1**). **Table 2** shows, however, that other income has nothing to do with operations and has no relation to Knudsen's construction business; it has mostly to do with securities, interest, and dividends. In 1994, the company's stock price was still in the $30 range. The company's directors, most with long-standing tenure on the board, expressed in the *Wall Street Journal* their amazement when Morrison Knudsen defaulted on its debt; they were apparently surprised at the financial condition of the company. The financials, however, were really quite clear about the declining percentage of earnings from operations. Recent examples of nonrecurring revenues include placing a gain on sale of asset components in "management services revenue," lengthening the period before bankruptcy charge-offs, and changing amortization schedules of marketing costs.

■ *SG&A expenses.* Interestingly, other income is often found in an examination of SG&A expenses. If SG&A is substantially lower than it has been in previous quarters, the company may have "hidden" a gain on sale in that account. Low interest expense is another cautionary item. Many companies add gain on sale as a reduction in interest income. The analyst must literally proceed line by line, comparing items with previous quarters and bringing outsized or undersized items to management's attention in the conference call.

## Balance Sheets

Balance sheets are difficult to obtain at the time of earnings releases; ideally, they would be faxed to analysts along with the income statement, but that is rarely the case. The conference call should include the usual questions regarding levels of inventory, receivables, prepaids, and other balance sheet accounts, focusing especially on year-over-year changes. The truly striking balance sheet problems require more preparation and tougher questions and can usually be grouped into one of eight categories:
- securities not marked to market;
- real estate at inflated values;
- inventories with obsolete products;
- receivables that have been booked too aggressively;

### Table 1. Morrison Knudsen's Income Statement, Year Ended December 31, 1991–93
($ thousands)

| Item | 1993 | 1992 | 1991 |
|---|---|---|---|
| Revenue | $2,722,543 | $2,284,931 | $2,024,791 |
| Cost of revenue | (2,646,081) | (2,233,624) | (1,942,877) |
| Operating income | 76,462 | 51,307 | 81,914 |
| General and administrative expenses | (37,358) | (38,160) | (48,813) |
| Research and development expenses | (3,701) | — | — |
| Gain on subsidiary sale of stock | 10,602 | — | — |
| Interest expense | (3,277) | (12,307) | (16,156) |
| Equity in net earnings (loss) and interest earned from unconsolidated affiliates | (5,757) | (133) | 5,545 |
| Other income, net | 25,827 | 23,676 | 35,964 |
| Income before income taxes, minority interests, extraordinary charge, and cumulative effect of accounting change | 62,798 | 24,383 | 58,454 |
| Income tax expense | (26,459) | (10,813) | (22,998) |
| Minority interests in net earnings of subsidiaries | (572) | (134) | — |
| Income before extraordinary charge and cumulative effect of accounting change | 35,767 | 13,436 | 35,456 |
| Extraordinary charge from write-off of unamortized debt issue, cost, net of tax | — | (3,096) | — |
| Cumulative effect of accounting change for postretirement health care costs, net of tax | — | (17,403) | — |

*Source*: Morrison Knudsen.

### Table 2. Morrison Knudsen's Other Income (Expense) Net, Year Ended December 31, 1991–93
($ thousands)

| Item | 1993 | 1992 | 1991 |
|---|---|---|---|
| Interest | $10,694 | $ 6,222 | $ 8,050 |
| Dividends | 2,733 | 10,860 | 9,371 |
| Gains on sales of marketable securities, net | 22,402 | 22,648 | 13,546 |
| Provisions for unrealized losses on marketable securities | (1,000) | (3,549) | — |
| Foreign currency transaction loss | — | (1,651) | — |
| Loss for terminating a nonconstruction joint venture | — | (1,475) | — |
| Loss on receivable sales | (3,578) | (3,184) | (516) |
| Underwriting expenses, net | (1,480) | (2,807) | (1,316) |
| Miscellaneous expenses, net | (3,944) | (3,388) | (345) |
| Gain on sale of corporate assets | — | — | 7,174 |
| Other income, net | $25,827 | $23,676 | $35,964 |

*Source*: Morrison Knudsen.

- receivables with loss provisions that are too low;
- bad loans;
- fuzzy, unbankable assets; and
- undocumented or unsupported accumulated depreciation.

The most troublesome balance sheet items are inventory, receivables, bad loans, and depreciation. Inventory is the single biggest indicator of problems for subsequent earnings.

*Inventory obsolescence.* Typically, inventory can include both obsolete inventory and expenses that a company is not expensing. Department 56 manufactures decorative Christmas houses and other giftware for retail sale. In April 1995, inventories were up 22 percent with cost of goods sold up 12 percent. In June, inventories were up 61 percent with cost of goods sold up 12 percent. The company explained that it had new product lines coming out. Of course, it is in the business of having new products and new lines come out continuously. The September quarter saw inventories up 87 percent and cost of goods sold up 12 percent. From early 1994 to the fall of 1995, the stock price rose from about $28 to about $45. Subsequent to the earnings shortfall, finally made visible in late 1995, the stock price fell into the low $20s for most of 1996. An investor could have acted at any of the inventory reporting points in 1995, even after the September inventory levels were known, and avoided all or nearly all of the loss.

■ *Accounts receivable.* Dramatic year-over-year increases in accounts receivable may mean that a company is booking revenues aggressively or is extending terms to attract new clients; such favorable terms should also result in, but often do not, a greater allowance for doubtful accounts. Quarterdeck Corporation's September 1995 quarter receivables were up 260 percent with sales up 142 percent. The company explained that the receivables were run up from shipping a new product. In the December quarter, receivables were up 490 percent with sales up 95 percent. In March, receivables were up 582 percent with sales up 53 percent. By that time, Quarterdeck should have been collecting on those sales, but it was not.

In June, Quarterdeck announced that the channel was full and sales would be down. At the same time, it also had negative cash flow, as most of these companies will when they have high receivables and inventories. The shareholders had every indicator of future stock price problems, which of course materialized with a vengeance. The Quarterdeck case also illustrates a particular difficulty in analyzing the receivables of high-tech companies, which typically will show receivable increases around new product releases. When is the increase no longer "normal"? Companies in the health care and medical industries also seem to be particularly prone to receivable run-ups. Two consecutive quarters of receivable run-ups almost always means that the reimbursement rate schedule has changed and an insurance company or the government is paying the company at lower levels than previously.

■ *Bad loans.* A recent disturbing, and growing, trend is for companies to lend money to quasi-captive companies so that the companies can pay management fees to the parent. An account on the balance sheet must be increasing as a result, but companies can be creative in hiding such loans. Some companies place the loan into long-term receivables, but many put it in other assets. In essence, they are lending nearly bankrupt companies the money to pay them fees; because the borrower is not a captive company, the lending company does not have to book the loss of the company it is lending money to, and most such lending companies do not create any allowance to offset the risk of these receivables. Current examples include two companies in the health care industry, one carrying both a loan and a defaulted bond in other assets and another lending money to franchisees in order to book real estate fees.

■ *Depreciation.* Often, companies do not detail depreciation on their income statements, so their balance sheets are the only source of depreciation information. Autotote Corporation's April 30, 1994, 10-Q provides a good illustration: Accumulated depreciation was $20.877 million, down from the prior quarter by $10 million. At the same time, property and equipment was up by $1 million quarter over quarter. A $10 million drop in accumulated depreciation for a company that earned approximately $26 million pretax was amazing, and the company was queried in a public meeting; it would give no disclosure on what the reversal was or why it was done. Analysts were left to draw their own conclusions, which was that Autotote had simply reversed earlier depreciation charges, perhaps by changing assumptions, and taken the benefit of the reversal into earnings. The stock price subsequently traded down from the $30s to the $1–$2 range.

## Conference Calls

In recent years, conference calls have become an important, perhaps essential, part of the earnings cycle. The primary rule to remember about conference calls is to stay on until the last question, because most companies seem to prioritize the questions according to who is on the line. They will typically take calls from an investment banker/analyst first, then from the most favorable analyst, then from their top shareholders, and then finally, after everybody has hung up out of boredom, from the short seller. These last questions just may be where the most learning takes place.

The objective of a conference call is to query the company about all the things that it did not disclose in the income statement and the balance sheet. Often, such disclosures come only in private calls to management because the level of detail is of no interest to other conference call participants, but open conference calls still provide much financial statement information. Tough questions are appropriate: What is the composition of such balance sheet accounts as other assets and prepaid expenses? What is operating cash flow? What are the inventory turnover targets? This sort of information in a public forum will let management know that somebody is paying attention to important financial detail. Often as important as the information itself is how the company answers questions and who answers questions. The level of seniority, the tone of voice, the detail and clarity of answers—all convey volumes about the company's willingness to get at earnings reality. The ideal responses will signal that earnings and prospective earnings are as anticipated, that management knows what is going on, and that the business is on course.

Examples of unproductive conference calls include the company that, upon suffering a major earnings problem, decided to both ask and answer the questions. One manager would ask about gross margins and another would answer.

Another company faced penetrating questions about a balance sheet account for unbilled long-term receivables and whether the resultant earnings were credible. In the conference call during this period of questioning, the company commented on scurrilous and slanderous attacks upon it by short sellers, and it said that it would sue them very shortly. It said that it had absolutely nothing to hide and that it would soon have an analysts' day, which would be by invitation only. About a year later, the company restated earnings, after pressure from its accountants, because it in fact had been booking revenues too aggressively; the stock traded down from about $30 to $9 over that year.

A third company's stock price dropped 20 percent on a Friday; during the conference call on Monday, the company's managers apologized for their somewhat disorganized response to the drop, indicating that they had all been attending a football game over the weekend. That certainly spoke volumes, positively or negatively depending on one's perspective, about the corporate culture.

## PORTFOLIO MAINTENANCE

Time pressures make portfolio maintenance particularly difficult to do properly. Three components of that maintenance—contacting management, studying 10-K and 10-Q reports, and monitoring interim announcements—are especially time-consuming but well worth the time spent.

## Contacting Management

Beyond the standard conference call, contacting management also involves management conversations and professional conferences. Management conversations are outside the public venue of a conference call. They involve one-on-one questioning on such topics as management's target gross and operating margins, its sales expectations in different business segments, its outlook for operating cash flow and return on invested capital, and its detailed financial statement analysis. Management responses provide tangible benchmarks to track every quarter.

Professional conferences are particularly good. Yes, the same companies make the same presentations over and over, but that is precisely the point; if the presentation changes, something real has changed. When a company quits being "a medical-practice management" company and starts being "an integrated health delivery" company, for instance, the likely reason is that its old strategic plan is not working. One company recently said in a meeting, when asked about pretax margins on a specific line of business, that it would not divulge that information, despite the fact that it had done so in previous meetings. The company said that it was not a margin company but a share company, that it managed by cash flow rather than by return on assets or return on equity. It operates in a very asset-intensive business, so these statements are certainly worrisome.

Contrast that behavior with the stance taken by another company that has had past problems but that states very publicly that analysts should be concerned if inventories or receivables grow more rapidly than sales or cost of goods sold. Which of the two management approaches suggests greater insight into balance sheet relationships and inspires greater confidence that management will deliver what it promises?

## Studying 10-Qs and 10-Ks

A second important aspect of portfolio maintenance is studying the financial documents, particularly the 10-Qs and 10-Ks. It is time-consuming, it is not exciting, but it will save many missteps in portfolio management. The best way to read these documents is side by side, comparing the previous 10-Q and the current 10-Q to see what changes the company has wrought.

**Table 3** shows six-month cash flow statements for Hollywood Entertainment Corporation, a video rental company. The company had positive cash flow of $14.1 million in the June 1995 quarter. Notice, however, that purchases of video rental inventory and purchases of property and equipment are about $46 million; for a company that rents movies, those purchases are a cost of doing business, which suggests an ongoing, substantial negative cash flow. Even more important is a "behind the scenes" transaction. In a portion of its 10-Q, Hollywood Entertainment disclosed that it bought a company, Video Watch. According to the agreement, the company could put its stock back to Hollywood Entertainment if Hollywood Entertainment's stock dropped below a certain level, a repurchase that, if consummated, would require Hollywood Entertainment to pay Video Watch nearly $52 million. This disclosure put a whole new light on Hollywood Entertainment's cash flow and on owning the stock. If the stock price was not going up, investors should worry. In fact, the stock price dropped and took the company's cash with it.

### Table 3. Hollywood Entertainment Consolidated Statements of Cash Flows, Six Months Ended June 30, 1994 and 1995
($ thousands)

|  | 1995 | 1994 |
|---|---|---|
| *Operating activities* | | |
| Net income | $ 5,530 | $ 2,527 |
| Adjustments to reconcile net income to cash provided by operating activities | | |
|   Depreciation and amortization | 17,218 | 6,963 |
|   Deferred rent and other liabilities | 396 | 265 |
|   Deferred income taxes | 1,141 | 238 |
| Changes in operating assets and liabilities | | |
|   Merchandise inventories | (654) | (411) |
|   Prepaid expenses and other current assets | (1,500) | (104) |
|   Accounts payable | (4,722) | 5,152 |
|   Accrued liabilities | (2,499) | 2,189 |
|   Income taxes payable | (749) | 530 |
|   Cash provided by operating activities | $ 14,161 | $ 17,349 |
| *Investing activities* | | |
| Receivables | (2,963) | (1,037) |
| Purchases of videocassette rental inventory, net | (27,696) | (9,350) |
| Purchases of property and equipment, net | (18,758) | (2,520) |
| Investment in businesses acquired | (6,810) | (53,480) |
| Other | (1,255) | 281 |
|   Cash used in investing activities | $(57,482) | $(66,106) |
| *Financing activities* | | |
| Proceeds from the issuance of common stock, net | — | 23,623 |
| Proceeds from long-term debt | 23,500 | 18,716 |
| Repayments of long-term debt | (11,043) | (112) |
| Tax benefit from exercise of stock options | 490 | — |
| Proceeds from exercise of stock options | 599 | — |
|   Cash provided by financing activities | 13,546 | 42,227 |
| Decrease in cash and cash equivalents | $(29,775) | $ (6,530) |
| Cash and cash equivalents | | |
|   Beginning of period | 39,017 | 9,605 |
|   End of period | $ 9,242 | $ 3,075 |

*Source*: Hollywood Entertainment 10-Q.

The MD&A section of Coastal Physician Group's 10-Q, excerpted below, is noteworthy for both its content and its timeliness:

> The Company will continue to seek methods of maintaining and improving its operating margins; however, a combination of factors could have an impact on the trend of operating margins. Overall market dynamics may lead to a reduced ability to obtain rate or premium increases in its hospital-based and managed-care businesses while having to respond to inflationary pressures from the physicians in the Company's integrated networks. Other factors include anticipated start-up losses of its recently licensed HMO in North Carolina, the costs of continued development of fee-for-service physician practices as a foundation for integrated delivery networks in selected markets, anticipated increases in competition in all markets, and continuing increases in price competition in its hospital-based services. Further, the Company expects to incur additional overhead costs for developing the necessary infrastructure to satisfy the increasing demand for its IPA [independent practice associations] management services and MSO [management services organizations] products. These factors, when coupled with the integration of its recent acquisitions and the changes in business mix during the past 12 months, may lead to some aberrations in operating margins in the near term. Additionally, the Company believes that legislated health care reform's effect, if any, on reimbursement levels could have an impact on the Company's trend of operating margins.

For the MD&A to admit that operating margins are going to deteriorate is very unusual; yet, a careful reading of the excerpt reveals that is exactly what management is saying. Management confirmed that interpretation in private conversations, pointing to substantial new competitive pressures as the reason for its caution. An investor acting on this 10-Q revelation at the time would have sold at what was practically the stock price high (low $30s range), just prior to the stock price tumbling steadily into the low single digits.

## Monitoring Interim Announcements

Most companies make interim announcements more or less continuously. Many are new product announcements, but it is important to determine that the company is not reannouncing the same product over and over. Similarly, an announcement of a new contract should be followed up, if necessary with both parties to the contract, to find out whether the implied scope and magnitude of the contract is actually true. For instance, a U.S. company announced a huge contract with a company in Mexico for a racetrack betting and lottery venture; the contract in reality was a very minor one for only a few machines rather than the multimillion dollar contract the U.S. company had implied.

Companies frequently make interim announcements to indicate that earnings will lag expectations for the quarter; in other words, the company announces in advance of the formal quarterly announcement that earnings will be disappointing. The key in this scenario is to determine whether the company will have many more quarters like this or whether it is a one-time problem that management has under control. Reappraising the financials and querying management, either in a conference call or privately, are certainly appropriate actions to take.

## SHORTCUTS

Although there is no substitute for the hard work involved in interpreting earnings announcements and in performing portfolio maintenance, some useful shortcuts—namely, computer databases and spreadsheets—help make those tasks, if not easier, at least more efficient.

## Computer Databases

Table 4 shows the major databases that are currently available. The three most important features of a database are

- quick access to frequently updated earnings estimates,
- balance sheet and income statement data by quarters for at least two years, and
- capability for screening by manipulation of the data.

The third feature is particularly important: For instance, the ability to screen either existing or potential stock holdings by receivables or inventory levels relative to sales or by operating cash flow levels relative to earnings, is truly timesaving. The problem is that those databases with the greatest capabilities are also the most expensive, often prohibitively so for many users.

## Spreadsheets

The second shortcut is having spreadsheets on all companies owned or followed. They are a necessity in three respects. First, inputing all the financial information, or checking someone else's input, is another check to assure that all the items on the balance sheet and income statement have been included and examined. Second, spreadsheets permit the generation of customized output specific to the needs and biases of the manager or analyst—all income statement items stated as a percent of sales, for instance, or both sequential and annual growth rates in income statement items, or inventory- and receivables-specific ratios. Whatever measures the user believes may be important in identifying potential anomalies for further study can be integrated into the spreadsheet. Third, spreadsheets are extremely useful in conferences and meetings with management. If management talks about improving margins or growing sales or increasing cash flow, the spreadsheet for that company contains the context and the history for those aspirations.

## CONCLUSION

When interpreting earnings announcements, consider the income statement, balance sheet, and conference call to be three indispensable tools. When

**Table 4. Comparison of Databases**

| Attribute | Compustat | First Call | Marketguide | FactSet |
|---|---|---|---|---|
| First Call estimates | Yes | Yes | Yes | Yes |
| Annual history | 20 years | 8 years | 14 years | 20 years |
| Quarterly history | 48 quarters | 20 quarters | 56 quarters | 44 quarters |
| Screening capabilities | Extensive | Extensive | Extensive | Extensive |
| Number of companies | 10,000+ | All publicly traded | 9,000 | 10,000+ |
| Update cycle | Daily and weekly | Daily | Daily and weekly | Daily and weekly |

*Source*: Gilder, Gagnon, Howe & Co., based on data from Compustat, First Call, Marketguide, and FactSet.

performing portfolio maintenance, contact management, study 10-Qs and 10-Ks, and monitor interim announcements. When searching for useful shortcuts, do not overlook computer databases and spreadsheets. This advice will not reduce the stress of a portfolio manager's or analyst's typical day, but at least it can make the search for earnings reality somewhat more manageable.

# Question and Answer Session

## Kathryn F. Staley, CFA

**Question:** Please discuss off-balance-sheet liabilities.

**Staley:** Off-balance-sheet liabilities, although much on our minds a few years ago, are much less of an issue in a sustained bull market. If you can print equity anytime you want to, why do you have to do anything funny? Nonetheless, when you are doing a detailed analysis of a 10-K, always read the debt section and look at the off-balance-sheet liabilities.

**Question:** Financial reporting in the various health care industries seems to be particularly troublesome. Is this symptomatic of the rapid growth and change in that business or of more deep-seated problems?

**Staley:** Health care is a huge target for both growth and change because it is such a huge percentage of our national economy. Thus, that industry seems also to be a tempting target for a number of fast operators. Accounting standards are also evolving along with the business, and my discussion of earnings announcements illustrates that the financial statements contain numerous "gray areas." You have to pay very careful attention to financial statements in the health care industry, especially to the receivables.

**Question:** In a conference call, how can you tell quickly whether you are witnessing a true earnings debacle or simply an aberrant quarter?

**Staley:** The only way that you can have a fair amount of confidence is if you have a long history of listening to management tell you what turns out to be the truth. If management has lied to me before, I am much more inclined to think "debacle," which is one reason I keep very careful notes of conference calls, meetings, and goals stated by management. I want to be able to say, "You told me last quarter that cash flow from operations would be positive." The only way I can do that is by documenting what was said in the past.

**Question:** Why would you have your clients' money invested in a stock when you have serious doubts about the integrity of that company's management?

**Staley:** One of the good things about earnings disasters is that they create opportunity in at least two ways. First, stocks can be driven so far below their fair value that, despite your suspicion that management has not been straightforward with you, you cannot in good conscience, or based on objective analysis, sell that stock. Second, times of management misinformation often are exactly when needed management changes occur; the company will bring in new people to rectify the situation.

# Reported Earnings for Multinational Corporations: The Impact of Currency Translation

Trevor S. Harris
*Kester and Byrnes Professor of Accounting and Auditing*
*Columbia University*

> The difficult task of making economic sense of reported earnings for a multinational company is complicated by ever-present currency effects. The nature and scope of foreign currency transactions, the foreign currency translation process, and the choice of functional currency—all dramatically affect company analysis and valuation.

Accounting is definitely not simple truth, and treating it as such is folly. This observation holds especially with foreign currency translation and, for that matter, any foreign-currency-related issue. "Globalization" is a trend that will continue, and in a global economy, foreign currency translation affects managers and investors, on both operating and financial levels. Translation practices differ not only among countries but also, even substantially, among companies and industries within the United States. Those who advocate simplifying those practices by "getting back to basics"—meaning revenues or cash flow—miss the point; foreign currency translation affects all relevant inputs, thus requiring keen understanding and thorough analysis.

This presentation illustrates the nature and effects of foreign currency transactions and foreign currency translation; addresses the importance of the choice of functional currency for multinational companies; and examines the impact of currency translation on company analysis and valuation.

## FOREIGN CURRENCY TRANSACTIONS

In the United States, to a large extent in the United Kingdom, and in countries adhering to evolving international accounting standards (IAS), all foreign-currency-related transactions are basically marked to market using the current exchange rate, with gains and losses—both realized and unrealized—included in reported income. Such treatment may be relatively new for other financial instruments, but it is a long-standing practice, especially in the United States, in the foreign currency arena.

Among other countries, various differences exist. Canadian practice, for instance, allows amortization of exchange gains and losses from foreign currency long-term loans. German law does not allow recognition of unrealized gains but requires recognition of unrealized losses. Japanese practice, although changing, has used historical exchange rates when translating long-term assets and liabilities. Contrary to U.S. practice, companies in many other countries are allowed to use forward rates for booking foreign currency transactions.

These considerations inevitably raise questions from the analyst's perspective. Exchange rate changes over time affect both operating and financial results in any multinational company. How are the forecasting process and the resulting projections influenced by these changes? How are basic operating statistics affected? What is the cost of making a product; what is the effect on pricing and on gross margins? Do the exchange rate gains and losses matter from a valuation point of view?

A simple example involving an inventory purchase confirms that these questions are not trivial. On September 30, 1995, Hedgehog, a U.S. company, purchased raw materials from a German manufacturer for DM2.18 million; the prevailing exchange rate was DM1.46/$1.00. Special financing terms allowed Hedgehog to make payment for the material on March 31, 1996. On December 31, 1995, Hedgehog's fiscal year-end, the exchange rate was DM1.40/$1.00, and on March 31, 1996, the exchange rate was DM1.56/$1.00. Hedgehog sold the goods containing the purchased raw materials for $1.8 million in cash on January 5, 1996.

Table 1 shows that, initially, the transaction would result in a $1.50 million increase in both inventory and accounts payable. On December 31, the purchase must be marked to market, resulting in a $60,000 increase in accounts payable. What becomes the offset to this increased liability? One option would be to add it to the cost of inventory that was not sold this year; that is, the increase in the marked-up payable is part of the cost of the goods the company is going to sell. In fact, U.S. accounting rules require that the increase in payables be recorded as a loss, which goes directly into the income statement.

To an analyst thinking about making an earnings forecast and treating this currency difference as part of the gross margin calculations, does this treatment result in a cost of goods sold of $1.50 million or $1.56 million? The right answer depends on what the analyst thinks is going to happen to the exchange rate. The company is going to have to replace that inventory from its German supplier; if the exchange rate stays at its current level, the margins for the forecasts would be overstated by using the $1.50 million figure.

In addition, Hedgehog now has a recorded loss, perhaps reported as operating, perhaps as nonoperating. The important question is whether this loss is a real loss to shareholders. Should the managers be held responsible? What could they have done? Had they paid the payable on September 30, that $60,000 loss would never have occurred. If they had paid it on December 31, they would have realized that $60,000 loss out of the cash account. In that respect, not paying the payable by year-end is a financing decision, but it is also a management decision, and some observers might argue that the managers chose to speculate on foreign exchange.

If that were the case, Table 1 shows that the managers' speculation was rewarded at the end of the next quarter, when the company actually did pay the amount owed. First, the inventory was sold for $1.80 million; given the cost of goods sold of $1.50 million, the company showed a gross margin of $300,000. Then, by the time of repayment on March 31, the dollar had appreciated, so Hedgehog realized a gain of $160,000 on the repayment. Thus, the picture at the end of the second quarter is completely different from at the end of the first, and that difference is the result of a conscious management decision. The overall net gain for the two quarters is $100,000, a very real gain that is now "sitting" in cash; granted, it is a one-time gain and any valuation multiple applied to it should reflect its nonrecurring nature. Nonetheless, management has generated cash that could go to the shareholders.

Hedgehog's experience shows that even a transaction as simple as a purchase of inventory requires caution on the part of analysts. These exchange gains and losses, which are generally not readily apparent in the financial statements, are real gains and losses. Applicable valuation multiples may be relatively low, because the gains and losses are not likely to recur, but that fact does not make their earnings effects less real.

## FOREIGN CURRENCY TRANSLATION

As with foreign currency transactions in general, foreign currency translation is a difficult issue, if only because of the effect of a company's choice of functional currency. In the so-called "functional currency" approach followed in the United States, the United Kingdom, and many other countries, companies look at what the operating currency is for a particular subsidiary. For instance, if the subsidiary is German, with sales, costs, and cash flows primarily in German marks, then the mark, the local currency, is defined as the functional currency. As a result, current exchange rates are used for translating German mark assets and liabilities into dollars, and

**Table 1. Accounting for Unhedged Foreign Currency Transactions: Hedgehog Company**
(US$ thousands)

| Date | Transaction | Cash | Inventory | Accounts Payable | Exchange Gain/(Loss) | Gross Profit |
|---|---|---|---|---|---|---|
| 9/30 | Purchase: DM2.184m/1.456 | | 1,500 | 1,500 | | |
| 12/31 | Exchange loss | | | 60 | (60) | |
| 12/31 | Balance: DM2.184m/1.40 | | 1,500 | 1,560 | (60) | |
| 1/5 | Inventory sold | 1,800 | | | | 1,800 |
|  | Cost of goods sold | | (1,500) | | | (1,500) |
| 3/31 | Repayment: DM2.184m/1.56 | (1,400) | | (1,560) | 160 | |
| Total | | 400 | 0 | 0 | 160 | 300 |

*Source*: Trevor S. Harris.

average exchange rates are used for translating German mark revenues, expenses, and gains or losses in order to consolidate the German subsidiary into the group accounts. In contrast, many German and Japanese companies would take a different approach, using, for instance, historical exchange rates for certain assets.

What should investors and analysts use? The importance of that question can be illustrated by a consolidation example; that is, what functional currency leads to economically relevant consolidated accounts?

## Functional Currency Alternatives

Table 2 presents the case of a U.S. company that owns a Swiss subsidiary, which in turn, owns a Swiss hotel that costs SFr67,500. The cost was financed with a SFr62,500 mortgage, and equity of $4,000 was provided by the U.S. parent on the original purchase date when the exchange rate was SFr1.25/$1.00. On the acquisition date, the dollar-denominated financial statement values, given in Column 4, would be the hotel asset of $54,000 (SFr67,500/1.25), the mortgage of $50,000 (SFr62,5000/1.25), and the $4,000 in equity.

Now, the task is to consolidate the subsidiary with the parent on the reporting date, when the exchange rate is SFr1.04/$1.00. Option A in Table 2 shows what would happen under strict historical cost accounting. The hotel is shown as $54,000, the loan as $50,000, and the equity as $4,000. Nothing has changed.

Option B shows how this example would differ if the U.S. dollar is viewed as the functional currency. The loan is marked to market (SFr62,500/1.04), giving a loan balance of $60,100. The historical U.S. dollar cost of the property is still $54,000, and the original investment is still $4,000, so the company records *a loss of $10,100*. Why does the financial obligation have to be marked to market? Because under this approach, the loan is treated as a foreign currency transaction and the company now owes $60,100.

Option C reflects the fact that this company is a Swiss company generating hotel rents in Swiss francs, paying its stock dividend in Swiss francs, and financing the mortgage in Swiss francs. Because this company is a Swiss franc company, the local currency becomes the functional currency, but the company still has to consolidate in dollars. Using the current exchange rate of 1.04, the asset is measured as $64,900, the loan is $60,100, and the equity, $4,000. Now, the company has *a gain of $800*.

For reporting in the year after the acquisition, does Option A, Option B, or Option C make most sense from an investor's point of view? Answers would vary. Few investors would argue that the subsidiary lost $10,100, and Option C is economically valid from a profitability perspective. But the choice of C can lead to a misleading inference about changes in the balance sheet account. For instance, the consolidated property value in dollars appears to have increased by 20 percent, from $54,000 to $64,900, since the time of acquisition. But no capital expenditure and no real value change need have occurred. Thus, the correct option for income and equity also creates misleading information in several of the line items.

Table 3 and Table 4 are built on the same conceptual idea as Options B and C in Table 2. In these examples, the U.S. parent purchased the shares in the Swiss subsidiary at a time when the exchange rate was SFr2.00/$1.00; at the reporting date, the exchange rate was SFr1.50/$1.00, so the average rate for the year was 1.75. Table 3 shows the balance sheets and income statements on a consolidated basis using the dollar as the functional currency, and Table 4 presents the same financial statements using the Swiss franc as the functional currency. Table 3 is essentially the same approach as in Option B of Table 2. It shows the exchange loss, $14,857, within the subsidiary. The effect on calculated return on equity (ROE) is remarkable. On the Swiss franc basis, the subsidiary's ROE is 37.5 percent, and for the holding company alone, the ROE is 33.3 percent. Application of this foreign currency translation approach, however, causes the consolidated ROE to be –45.3 percent.

### Table 2. Consolidation of a Foreign Subsidiary

| Equity/Liability | Swiss Franc | Exchange Rate (SFr per $) | Dollar Values at Acquisition | Dollar Values after Acquisition |||
|---|---|---|---|---|---|---|
| | | | | Option A | Option B | Option C |
| Hotel (asset) | 67,500 | 1.25 | $54,000 | $54,000 | $54,000 | $64,900 |
| Loan | 62,500 | 1.25 | 50,000 | 50,000 | 60,100 | 60,100 |
| Equity before gain/(loss) | 5,000 | 1.25 | 4,000 | 4,000 | 4,000 | 4,000 |
| Gain/(loss) | 0 | | 0 | 0 | (10,100) | 800 |
| Total equity and liability | 67,500 | | $54,000 | $54,000 | $54,000 | $64,900 |

*Source*: Trevor S. Harris.

### Table 3. Consolidating Accounts with U.S. Dollar as Functional Currency

| Account | Subsidiary Company (SFr) | Exchange Rate (SFr per $) | Subsidiary Company (US$) | Holding Company (US$) | Total (US$) | Adjustment (US$) | Group (US$) |
|---|---|---|---|---|---|---|---|
| *Balance sheet* | | | | | | | |
| Cash | 3,000 | 1.5 | $ 2,000 | $ 7,000 | $ 9,000 | | $ 9,000 |
| Property | 98,000 | 2.0 | 49,000 | 49,000 | 98,000 | | 98,000 |
| Investment | | | | 4,000 | 4,000 | $(4,000) | 0 |
| Total assets | 101,000 | | $51,000 | $60,000 | $111,000 | $(4,000) | $107,000 |
| Debt | 90,000 | 1.5 | 60,000 | 40,000 | 100,000 | | 100,000 |
| Capital | 8,000 | 2.0 | 4,000 | 15,000 | 19,000 | (4,000) | 15,000 |
| Retained earnings | 3,000 | | (13,000) | 5,000 | (8,000) | | (8,000) |
| Total equity and liability | 101,000 | | $ 51,000 | $60,000 | $111,000 | $(4,000) | $107,000 |
| *Income statement* | | | | | | | |
| Revenue | 17,500 | 1.75 | $ 10,000 | $15,000 | | | $ 25,000 |
| Depreciation | (2,000) | 2.00 | (1,000) | (1,000) | | | (2,000) |
| Interest | (8,750) | 1.75 | (5,000) | (4,000) | | | (9,000) |
| Other | (1,750) | 1.75 | (1,000) | (2,000) | | | (3,000) |
| Exchange loss | | | (14,857) | | | | (14,857) |
| Tax | (2,000) | 1.75 | (1,143) | (3,000) | | | (4,143) |
| Net income | 3,000 | | $(13,000) | $ 5,000 | | | $ (8,000) |
| Return on equity | 37.5% | | (325%) | 33.3% | | | (45.3%) |

*Source*: Trevor S. Harris.

Table 4, which essentially mirrors Option C of Table 2, shows positive ROE levels across the board. The parent and subsidiary ROEs are identical to those in Table 3, but now the consolidated ROE is 44.8 percent, contrasted with the –45.3 percent in Table 3. The method of currency translation has made all the difference in the reported results; nothing else has changed.

### Functional Currency Choices

Given that choice of functional currency clearly affects reported earnings, part of an analyst's job is to determine what functional currency a company has chosen. In fact, examining just three industries reveals that even companies within the same industry make different choices, so that part of the analytical process becomes even more important.

### Table 4. Consolidating Accounts with Swiss Franc as Functional Currency

| Account | Subsidiary Company (SFr) | Exchange Rate (SFr per $) | Subsidiary Company (US$) | Holding Company (US$) | Total (US$) | Adjustment (US$) | Group (US$) |
|---|---|---|---|---|---|---|---|
| *Balance sheet* | | | | | | | |
| Cash | 3,000 | 1.5 | $ 2,000 | $ 7,000 | $ 9,000 | | $ 9,000 |
| Property | 98,000 | 1.5 | 65,333 | 49,000 | 114,333 | | 114,333 |
| Investment | | | | 4,000 | 4,000 | $(4,000) | 0 |
| Total assets | 101,000 | | $67,333 | $60,000 | $127,333 | $(4,000) | $123,333 |
| Debt | 90,000 | 1.5 | 60,000 | 40,000 | 100,000 | | 100,000 |
| Capital | 8,000 | 1.5 | 5,333 | 15,000 | 20,333 | (5,333) | 15,000 |
| Retained earnings | 3,000 | | 1,713 | 5,000 | 6,713 | | 6,713 |
| Translation adjustment | | | 287 | | 287 | 1,333 | 1,620 |
| Total equity and liability | 101,000 | | $67,333 | $60,000 | $127,333 | $(4,000) | $123,333 |
| *Income statement* | | | | | | | |
| Revenue | 17,500 | 1.75 | $10,000 | $15,000 | | | $ 25,000 |
| Depreciation | (2,000) | 1.75 | (1,144) | (1,000) | | | (2,144) |
| Interest | (8,750) | 1.75 | (5,000) | (4,000) | | | (9,000) |
| Other | (1,750) | 1.75 | (1,000) | (2,000) | | | (3,000) |
| Exchange loss | | | | | | | (4,143) |
| Tax | (2,000) | 1.75 | (1,143) | (3,000) | | | |
| Net income | 3,000 | | $(1,713) | $ 5,000 | | | $ (6,713) |
| Return on equity | 37.5% | | (43%) | 33.3% | | | (44.8%) |

*Source*: Trevor S. Harris.

■ *Computer companies.* Should IBM Corporation, Digital Equipment Corporation, and Hewlett-Packard Company, all following U.S. generally accepted accounting principles (GAAP), use Option B or Option C? IBM has large operations in Japan and Germany. Hewlett-Packard has production and sales facilities in Japan and Germany. Digital has most of its production facilities in the United States, but both Digital and IBM generate about 70 percent of their sales outside the United States. In other words, all three U.S. companies have substantial nondomestic operations or nondomestic sales, so each might choose either the dollar or the local currency as the functional currency, and all three might well be expected to make similar decisions.

In fact, IBM uses local currency as the functional currency, but Digital and Hewlett-Packard use the dollar. Although most U.S. and U.K. companies use local currency as the functional currency, an analyst cannot merely assume that all companies in an industry, even ones as similar in non-U.S. scope as IBM and Hewlett-Packard, will choose the same functional currency.

■ *Oil and gas conglomerates.* Oil and gas conglomerates are particularly interesting; because oil is a product that is priced worldwide in dollars, the point of sale is irrelevant. So, do oil and gas conglomerates consistently choose the dollar as their functional currency? Exxon Corporation basically uses local currency as the functional currency but switches for certain of its operations, sometimes using the dollar and sometimes local currency. Chevron Corporation, by contrast, uses the dollar exclusively.

■ *Pharmaceuticals.* Merck & Company, Johnson & Johnson, and Warner-Lambert Company have production facilities and R&D efforts outside the United States. Each company, although having its own idiosyncrasies, might well be expected to choose the same functional currency approach, and in fact, most pharmaceuticals, including Johnson & Johnson and Warner-Lambert, use local currency as the functional currency. Merck uses the dollar as the functional currency but is well known for having high-quality foreign exchange management.

## DOES FOREIGN CURRENCY TRANSLATION MATTER?

Do the choices made by these companies make a difference in reported returns? **Table 5** and **Table 6** suggest strongly that they do indeed matter. Table 5 shows that IBM's reported income for 1994 is about $3 billion before the foreign currency translation adjustment. Using local currency as the functional currency adds another $1 billion; in 1994, the dollar was generally depreciating. By adding in that $1 billion,

**Table 5. Foreign Currency Translation: Impact on EPS and Return on Common Equity for IBM**

| Item | 1995 | 1994 |
|---|---|---|
| Reported income (US$ billions) | 4,116 | 2,937 |
| Translation adjustment (US$ billions) | 364 | 1,014 |
| Adjusted income (US$ billions) | 4,480 | 3,951 |
| Reported EPS (US$) | 7.23 | 5.02 |
| Adjusted EPS (US$) | 7.87 | 6.75 |
| Reported beginning equity (US$ billions) | 23,413 | 19,738 |
| Reported return on common equity | 17.6% | 14.9% |
| Adjusted return on common equity | 19.1% | 20.0% |

*Source*: Trevor S. Harris.

**Table 6. Foreign Currency Translation: Impact on EPS and Return on Common Equity for the Nestlé Group**

| Item | 1994 | 1993 |
|---|---|---|
| Reported income (US$ billions) | 3,250 | 2,887 |
| Translation adjustment (US$ billions) | (1,778) | (1,248) |
| Adjusted income (US$ billions) | 1,472 | 1,639 |
| Reported EPS (US$) | 83.7 | 76.5 |
| Adjusted EPS (US$) | 37.4 | 42.6 |
| Reported beginning equity (US$ billions) | 15,660 | 13,930 |
| Reported return on common equity | 20.8% | 20.7% |
| Adjusted return on common equity | 9.3% | 11.8% |

*Source*: Trevor S. Harris.

earnings per share (EPS) increased from $5.02 to $6.75, or by about 34 percent. Similarly, the ROE increased from approximately 15 percent to 20 percent—a different picture of profitability. In 1995, the translation adjustment was much smaller, although still between 8 and 9 percent of reported income.

An even starker example is the Nestlé Group, shown in Table 6. Nestlé's corporate strategy was to fund all long-term assets outside Switzerland with Swiss franc equity. For example, it funded the purchase of Carnation by investing Swiss franc equity. The result was that in 1993, the translation adjustment was more than 43 percent of the company's earnings for the year; in 1994, the translation adjustment was nearly 55 percent of reported net income. The effect on ROE is striking. An analyst could argue that Nestlé's ROE for the two years was consistent at about 21 percent or that Nestlé's ROE dropped from about 12 percent to about 9 percent. The argument rests on whether the reported or adjusted results are more valid.

Are these results relevant to investors? Should they think of IBM's cumulative translation adjustment of more than $1.3 billion as a real addition to value? Did Nestlé actually destroy more than $3.0 billion of value for its shareholders? Option C, using the local currency as the functional currency, implies that investors should care very much about this matter, that the adjustment is a real increase or decrease in value for the shareholder. The implication rests on the use of the local currency for financing purposes. If Nestlé had funded its acquisition with local debt and SFr1.00 in equity or if IBM used local debt and $1.00 in equity, the translation adjustment differences would disappear but would be replaced by an interest charge. The effect of that financing strategy would certainly be seen as real, in that both the operating results and the equity position would be altered. The effects in Tables 5 and 6 are no less real; valuation multiples might be different from what they are in the presence of interest charges, if only because the translation adjustments would not be expected to recur, but value has changed, clearly and measurably. The only way to argue that these are not value changes is to contend that the exchange rate movements that gave rise to the adjustments will reverse themselves perfectly. Few analysts or managers would pursue that argument.

## FOREIGN CURRENCY TRANSLATION AND COMPANY ANALYSIS

If translation effects do, or should, matter to investors, then the impact of those effects should be stressed in the valuation process, particularly in forecasting cash flows and measuring business activity.

### Cash Flow Translation

Many analysts would argue that all these issues amount to no more than "accounting shenanigans" that would be eliminated by a sole focus on cash flow. In fact, cash flow translation helps little.

**Table 7** shows a Swiss subsidiary's cash account that has a beginning balance of SFr10,100 on January 1. Two cash flows occur: an inflow of SFr10,030 and an outflow of SFr10,800, resulting in a negative cash flow of SFr770.00. The question is which cash flows should be the focus for valuation purposes. A related issue is how the subsidiary's cash flows should be translated into U.S. dollars for incorporation in the consolidated cash flow statement, which most analysts see.

In Option 1, the cash account begins at $9,100, based on the January 1 exchange rate; the account balance is $8,800 at the end, based on the March 31 exchange rate. This negative cash flow of $300 is the change in the cash balance that, under U.S. accounting rules, must be reconciled in the cash flow statements. Thus, the Option 1 treatment recognizes the change in the beginning and ending cash balances in dollars. Option 2 requires using the exchange rate on the dates when these cash flows occurred. So, the SFr10,030 becomes $9,200 and the SFr10,800 becomes $9,000, a gain in dollars that will be reported as a positive operating cash flow of $200. This amount, reconciled to the negative $300, results in an exchange loss of $500. Option 3 divides the negative SFr770 cash flow by the March 31 rate, producing a negative cash flow of about $733. This amount, in turn, reconciled with the negative $300, results in an exchange gain of $433.

From a valuation perspective that involves forecasting and discounting cash flows, which option should be used? Option 1, which portrays the change in the cash balance as simply being –$300, is misleading as a measure of the change in actual cash. Option 2, which is U.S. GAAP, IAS, U.K. GAAP, and any other approach that incorporates a cash flow statement based on GAAP, indicates a cash flow of positive $200 when cash is actually flowing out of the company. Option 2 is also patently unrealistic; the only circumstance that would replicate that same cash flow in a floating-exchange-rate environment would be perfect correlation between the rate of flow in local currency and the rate of change in exchange rates, and that will never happen in any real business environment. Option 3 is the most plausible from the standpoint of economic reality; the real cash flow is –SFr770, and the U.S. dollar measure that reflects this most closely is the –$733 given by Option 3 (although even Option 3 may lead to inappropriate interpretations if the $733 loss is not realized).

The example can be extended to noncash accounts, and the potential for misinterpreting true cash flow is clearly high. Even the negative change in

**Table 7. Foreign Currency Translation: Example of Cash Flow Translation**

| Date/Item | SFr Cash | Exchange Rate (SFr per $) | Option 1 Δ Dollar Cash | Option 2 Conversion (US$) | Option 3 Δ SFr Cash |
|---|---|---|---|---|---|
| January 1 | 10,010 | 1.10 | 9,100 | 9,100 | |
| February 10 | 10,030 | 1.09 | NA | 9,200 | |
| March 1 | (10,800) | 1.20 | NA | (9,000) | |
| March 31 actual | 9,240 | 1.05 | 8,800 | 8,800 | |
| Cash flow | (770) | | (300) | 200 | (733) |
| Change in cash balances | (770) | | (300) | (300) | (300) |
| Exchange gain/(loss) | 0 | | 0 | (500) | 433 |

*Source*: Trevor S. Harris.

the cash balance of $300 is misleading as a measure of the change in actual cash.

Thus, one of the lessons of Table 7 is that all traditional cash flow measures actually seen by analysts are problematic at best and potentially useless at worst.

## Measuring Business Activity

Translation effects are not limited to consolidated net income, equity, or cash flow. Other measures of business activity, such as sales and gross margins, are also affected by currency translation, and company comparisons invite cautious scrutiny of the translation impact.

IBM's 1995 annual report, for instance, indicated that currency rate variations had a 2 percent favorable effect on revenue in the fourth quarter and a 4 percent favorable effect for all of 1995; the currency contribution had previously been 2 percent positive for 1994 and 3 percent negative for 1993. These contributions should not be surprising in light of the fact that more than 60 percent of IBM's sales are outside the United States.

In contrast, Digital's 1996 10-K report indicated that the net effect of exchange rate movements on revenues was insignificant in fiscal 1996 compared with 1995 and positive in fiscal 1995 compared with 1994. Well over 60 percent of Digital's sales are outside the United States, but Digital also uses a different functional currency from that of IBM.

Given these apparent divergent effects for such similar companies, how are gross margins, and financial reporting in general, affected by currency translation? **Table 8** portrays a German subsidiary of a U.S. parent that for each of three quarters has DM1.50 million in sales and DM1 million in costs. The exchange rate was DM1.5/$1.00 in Quarter 1 and DM1.35 in Quarters 2 and 3. For the second and third quarters, because of the exchange rate movement, the subsidiary's cost of sales and operating profit increased 11 percent compared with Quarter 1. Treating that as "real" sales growth and applying a corresponding valuation multiple to it or to the resulting operating margin would be a serious mistake; that growth is not operating growth, and that rate of growth is not sustainable.

What if the subsidiary passes through at least some of the exchange rate change into changes in the selling price? **Table 9** assumes the same 10 percent change in the exchange rate at the beginning of Quarter 2, but the subsidiary's second- and third-quarter sales increase to DM1.575 million because of a 5 percent increase in the selling price. German mark sales increased, but the costs remained the same. With the currency effect still at work, analysis becomes decidedly more difficult. Sales now reflect a multiplier effect from both the currency effect and the price increase, and sales increase nearly 17 percent from the second to third quarters. With costs only rising 11 percent, the operating profit increases 28 percent. From a short-term valuation perspective, this change may be good news, but again it is not sustainable, probably not even into the third quarter.

**Table 10** reflects the same conditions as Table 9 except that the exchange rate change from DM1.50 to DM1.35 occurs in the middle of the second quarter, so the average exchange rate for Quarter 2 is DM1.45.

Table 8. Foreign Currency Translation: Effects of End-of-Period Change in Exchange Rates
(US$ thousands except as noted)

| Item | 1Q | 2Q | Percent Change | 3Q | Percent Change |
|---|---|---|---|---|---|
| Sales | $1,000 | $1,111 | 11.1 | $1,111 | 0 |
| Cost of sales | 667 | 741 | 11.1 | 741 | 0 |
| Operating profit | 333 | 370 | 11.1 | 370 | 0 |
| Operating margin | 33.3% | 33.3% |  | 33.3% |  |

*Source*: Trevor S. Harris.

Table 9. Foreign Currency Translation: Combined Effects of End-of-Period Change in Exchange Rates and Increase in Selling Price
(US$ thousands except as noted)

| Item | 1Q | 2Q | Percent Change | 3Q | Percent Change |
|---|---|---|---|---|---|
| Sales | $1,000 | $1,167 | 16.7 | $1,167 | 0 |
| Cost of sales | 667 | 741 | 11.1 | 741 | 0 |
| Operating profit | 333 | 426 | 27.8 | 426 | 0 |
| Operating margin | 33.3% | 36.5% |  | 36.5% |  |

*Source*: Trevor S. Harris.

Now, the combined effects of the exchange rate change and the price increase linger through both the second and third quarters; the operating measures all end up at the same levels as in Table 9, but the changes are more gradual, occurring over two quarters. The same cautions about valuation and sustainability, however, certainly apply.

Tables 8 through 10 impart an important lesson: Analysis, projections, and valuations involving multinational corporations require a thorough understanding of the sources of apparent operating results. Is the company reporting real operating results or currency-induced effects? Currency effects are not likely to be sustainable for any length of time and should not draw the same valuation multiples as operating results.

## CONCLUSION

Foreign currency transactions and translation have the potential to seriously distort earnings analysis and the valuation process. What can analysts and investors do?

- Understand the sources of costs and revenues; sources make a difference with respect to sustainability and valuation multiples, and differentiation between the currency component and the true underlying business is critical.
- Know how assets are denominated and how those assets are financed.
- Project revenues, costs, and cash flows within a country or region; although this proposition can be intimidating, most multinational companies, in fact, generate most of their business in only a few countries or regions.

With respect to analysis and valuation of multinational companies in general, two larger lessons seem to arise from these observations:

- Any kind of aggregate analysis is very dangerous.
- There is no substitute for careful, fundamental analysis of corporate structure and operations.

**Table 10. Foreign Currency Translation: Combined Effects of Midperiod Change in Exchange Rates and Increase in Selling Price**
(US$ thousands)

| Item | 1Q | 2Q | Percent Change | 3Q | Percent Change |
|---|---|---|---|---|---|
| Sales | $1,000 | $1,086 | 8.6 | $1,167 | 7.4 |
| Cost of sales | 667 | 690 | 3.4 | 741 | 7.4 |
| Operating profit | 333 | 396 | 18.9 | 426 | 7.4 |
| Operating margin | 33.3% | 36.5% | | 36.5% | |

*Source*: Trevor S. Harris.

# Understanding Global Accounting Practices and Standards

David F. Hawkins
*Professor of Business Administration*
*Harvard University Graduate School of Business*

> Sorting out the earnings implications of accounting practices and standards in a global context requires astute analysis indeed. Current developments in the evolution of international accounting standards address a variety of serious financial reporting problems that investors encounter in using non-U.S. financial statements.

The search for economic reality in reported earnings inevitably involves the analysis of financial reports, which are driven by prevailing accounting practices and standards. Sorting out the implications of those practices and standards in a domestic-only setting is difficult enough, but doing so in a global context requires even more effort, knowledge, and skill. This presentation addresses current developments in the evolution of international accounting standards (IAS) and examines a variety of serious financial reporting problems that investors encounter in using financial statements from non-U.S. companies, many of which are being addressed by the evolving IAS.

## THE EVOLUTION AND USE OF IAS

Historically, for a number of good reasons, U.S. investors have had very little interest in IAS. First, the standards have not covered all of the accounting issues typically raised by corporate financial reports. Second, most IAS were not the "highest and best practice" but, rather, reflected the lowest common denominator of accounting practice among the representatives of the world's professional accounting bodies who were members of the International Accounting Standards Committee (IASC). Thus, the rules have tended to be broad generalizations that allow managements a huge amount of judgment in interpretation and application. They were, in many instances, ambiguous and even contradictory. Third, IAS had no authority behind them. There was no mechanism for enforcement and no way of getting companies to apply IAS, at least as the drafters had intended them to be applied.

Fortunately, the role and accounting quality of IAS are now changing very rapidly. These changes could generate substantial new interest in IAS on the part of U.S. investors.

The IASC has reached agreement with the International Organization of Securities Commissions (IOSCO), which is an association for the various securities and exchange commissions around the world. (The U.S. SEC is a very important member of IOSCO.) That agreement specified that if by March 1998, the IASC could come up with a core set of standards of sufficient quality that is acceptable to the IOSCO, then the IOSCO would adopt those standards for cross-border listings around the world.

The success of the IASC–IOSCO agreement would enable investors to "cast a wider net" (that is, consider a greater number of non-U.S. company equities). The IASC is already well under way on this project. In the meantime, the move toward acceptance of IAS outside of this agreement is proceeding at a decidedly fast but uneven pace. Today, for instance, companies can list using IAS in any country in the world except Canada, Japan, and the United States. The European Commission, the group charged with setting accounting standards for the European Community, has decided it will not adopt European standards but will instead adopt IAS. Within the European Community, different countries have different stances. France is moving toward IAS. It will give listed companies "a free choice" to use IAS, U.S. generally accepted accounting principles (GAAP), U.K. GAAP, or French GAAP in consolidated statements. Germany is taking a similar step, and as a result, many of the major German companies will be using IAS by the end of 1997. U.K. accounting, also widely used in Europe, is already very similar to IAS, but some major exceptions include goodwill and income tax accounting.

Many of the emerging market countries of the world are moving away from their local accounting heritages and toward IAS. For instance, China will have accounting standards based on IAS by the end of 1997. The Confederation of Independent States, during 1997, will adopt at least some accounting practices based on IAS. The former U.K. colonies are moving away from U.K. GAAP to IAS. Even Mexico, which has used U.S. GAAP for years, is now going to IAS in areas that Mexican GAAP does not cover.

The IOSCO will likely adopt the core IAS standards. The U.S. SEC has stated that it will not insist on the IAS being the same as U.S. GAAP or on the IAS-based statements being reconciled to U.S. GAAP. It will, however, insist that the IAS be capable of being applied rigorously; that is, different companies will be able to apply IAS to the same transaction and get the same accounting results.

I believe that the IASC will meet the IOSCO–SEC requirements. As a result, non-U.S. companies will most likely be listing on U.S. exchanges in a few years using IAS, and those U.S. investors who take the trouble to understand IAS will realize substantial benefits. Their newfound IAS knowledge might well encourage and enable them to venture beyond U.S.-only listings to consider other parts of the world, because the analytical costs associated with looking at non-U.S. companies will fall dramatically. If investors learn about IAS, they will be able, probably in a year or two, to feel very confident from the accounting point of view about looking at listed companies in a whole host of non-U.S. markets. At the same time, those non-U.S. stocks will become increasingly liquid as they become known to a wider and more knowledgeable audience.

## FINANCIAL REPORTING PROBLEMS

Financial analysts are interested in predicting earnings and dividends. In that context, financial statements that are not based on U.S. GAAP are often extremely difficult to use in a number of respects. The new and projected IAS address a number of those difficulties.

■ *Interim statements.* Analysts rely heavily on interim statements. U.S. GAAP provides for interim statements, but few other countries have local GAAP that result in meaningful interim statements. Overseas, these statements typically are issued every six months, usually long after the events they document have occurred. Also, when some overseas companies prepare interim statements, many of them feel free to smooth earnings, make allocations between periods, and defer items from one period to another.

The IASC has proposed that statements for each interim period must stand on their own. Companies cannot defer items they could not defer at the annual period. They cannot allocate items they would not allocate in their annual reports. This "independent theory" says that a period of accounting is a period of accounting—a tough-minded approach. Even if some unusual episode devastates earnings in the current interim period, the company must report it that period; it cannot smooth its earnings. This change will be a major one that investors should welcome.

■ *Segment reporting.* Another important area of analyst interest is business-segment reporting. Many companies outside the United States do not report business-segment data, and many of those that do report segment data report information that is limited to sales. To the extent that companies do more complete segment reporting, they follow the U.S. pattern, namely, reporting segments comprising activities that have common risk–reward characteristics. The problem with that approach is that companies keep changing the definition of those segments, so no constant history of like segments is available.

Now, a joint effort is under way involving the IASC, the U.S. Financial Accounting Standards Board (FASB), and the Canadian Institute of Chartered Accountants to move to a new approach to segment reporting. This approach is to report the same disaggregated business data that a CEO looks at when he or she allocates resources, which is known as the management unit approach to segment reporting. The theory is that managers are not going to tamper with the way they manage their companies in order to make segment information confusing. This change would be a real step forward in that it would impart more stability over time to segment definitions and thus be more useful to analysts.

■ *Earnings per share (EPS).* Another problem is the reporting of EPS. Outside the United States, most countries do not even define EPS, so practices differ widely. Whenever an analyst sees a non-U.S. company reporting EPS, that analyst's first task is to find out how EPS was calculated. A Brazilian company, for example, probably uses the shares outstanding at the end of the year as the denominator. A U.K. company will probably provide the official EPS calculations, but the one that will catch your attention, the "headline EPS," is the one management invents. U.K. companies are allowed, if they do not like their official EPS numbers, to provide what they believe are "truer and fairer" calculations. The Japanese EPS approach does not use a weighted-average number of shares but, rather, an average of the shares at the beginning and the end of the year, and options and warrants that have expired during the year are not included in the EPS calculations. Past EPS calculations are not restated to reflect stock splits and stock dividends. The point is that, currently, an analyst must look at local EPS rules carefully—if such rules exist.

The IASC and the FASB are addressing the EPS problem. They are about to come up with a global EPS approach. In the near future, the EPS calculation, even in the United States, will be substantially different. In the United States, primary EPS will be dropped and replaced by basic EPS, which is net income less preferred stock dividends divided by a weighted average of the number of common shares outstanding. Fully diluted EPS will be renamed diluted EPS. It will be a far simpler calculation using the "if converted" and "treasury stock" methods.

■ *Pensions.* Companies overseas use a wide range of actuarial valuation approaches; no particular standard has been adopted. Thus, pensions in the global context have been very difficult to deal with; analysts, by themselves, cannot unravel the methodology and are not equipped to judge non-U.S. companies that have large pension or other employee-benefit obligations.

The IASC is about to propose that all companies use one actuarial method to compute pension obligations, as companies do in the United States. Regardless of which method is chosen, such a change certainly will be an improvement over current practice.

■ *Asset impairments.* Asset impairment reporting has been a substantial problem for analysts because non-U.S. companies take the position that they will not write down an impaired asset unless they believe the impairment is permanent. Who can make that kind of judgment? The result of such a stance is that a company will write an asset down when it feels like writing it down.

The IASC is moving toward requiring that a company write down an asset when the company believes the present value of the related future cash flows is less than the carrying value. This type of approach has the advantage of being quantifiable and of allowing analysts to ask company managements some hard questions about asset values.

■ *Discontinued operations.* Most countries do not have rules on how to account for discontinued operations. The key questions in reporting discontinued operations are when the discontinuance should be reported and what the reporting should include. In many countries, companies wait until an operation is absolutely discontinued. Other countries say companies should start accounting for a discontinuance when the decision to discontinue is made.

The IASC will likely specify a fixed rule aimed at eliminating alternative ways of treating the same transaction. For instance, when a company commits and cannot back out of discontinuing an operation, the company should start showing it as a discontinued operation.

■ *Provisions and contingencies.* Outside the United States, the attitude toward setting up provisions for contingencies is very different from that in the United States. If a non-U.S. company has a good year, it puts some of its profits into provisions. If it has a bad year, it pulls some earnings out of its contingency reserves. The goal is to smooth earnings; the company would not want anybody to think it is in trouble in a bad year or that it should raise dividends because times are good. Such companies argue that they are taking a long perspective, but unless these provisions and changes in them are fully disclosed, analysts cannot know whether they are looking at reality.

The IASC will likely issue a statement in the near future that says companies should set up contingency provisions when they have an obligation to transfer economic resources that exist as of the date of the statements. The word "obligation" implies that the transfer is going to be real, not illusory or imaginary. A company cannot simply say that it needs to provide for contingencies even though it has no reason now to set up such a reserve other than it simply wants to put something away for a rainy day. That action has been permitted historically but most probably will not be under IAS in the future.

■ *Intangible assets.* The accounting treatment of intangible assets varies greatly among countries. The British, Australians, and Dutch allow companies to put on their balance sheets "brand" values that were internally generated and acquired. This practice is never allowed in the United States. One can argue, however, that these assets are real and, therefore, ought to be taken into account in looking at company data.

The IASC will most likely say that companies cannot put such intangibles on their balance sheets unless an active secondary market exists for those assets. That argument will be a "tough sell," however, because it tries to eliminate a practice that some people think reflects economic reality.

The problem that brand values present is reliability. The goal of accounting is to reflect economic reality, but accounting must also recognize the problem of reliable measurements. How are brand values measured? Where do the brand values come from? How reliable are the fairness letters that now so often accompany brand-value estimates? The IASC has examined these questions and concluded that the accounting treatment of brand values is best left up to a market test.

Intangible assets, of course, also include goodwill, which is a major problem around the world. In many countries, companies are allowed to write off goodwill at acquisition.

The IASC has already ended this practice. The major Swiss companies, for example, no longer write off goodwill at acquisition, because they follow IAS. The British and the Germans still do write goodwill off at acquisition, but the IAS position that goodwill must be capitalized and written off over a period not to exceed 20 years has put these two countries under pressure to change their own rules. The U.K. response has been to try to convince the IASC to adopt a rule requiring goodwill to be capitalized and subjected to a periodic impairment test. The signs are that the U.K. proposal may prevail.

■ *Financial instrument disclosures.* Derivatives pose a problem that neither the IASC nor the FASB has solved. They represent a great black accounting hole overseas. Disclosures have been very poor.

The IASC has come up with standards that call for improved disclosures. They are comparable to U.S. standards on disclosures. Nevertheless, analysts still have great difficulty knowing how people elsewhere in the world are accounting for derivatives.

■ *Income taxes.* Deferred tax accounting can make a huge difference in a company's reported performance in various parts of the world. At least four different ways of accounting for deferred income taxes are practiced. In Japan, companies do not account for them. U.K. companies can use partial tax allocation, showing only deferred taxes they think are going to be paid in the next three to five years, a judgment call. Other countries use the liability method, which bases deferred taxes on book–tax balance sheet differences. Many other countries use the deferral method, which bases deferred taxes on book pretax income and taxable income.

The IASC has just issued a new standard that says companies must account for all differences between book and tax accounting. This procedure is known as comprehensive tax allocation. It eliminates accounting practices that perhaps have some justification. The partial tax allocation approach, for instance, has economic reality on its side: Why provide for something you will never have to pay? IAS, however, are mainly designed to eliminate accounting differences, and the IAS approach to deferred taxes reflects that goal, in that most countries have rejected partial tax allocation.

## OTHER REPORTING PROBLEMS

In addition to the financial reporting problems that IAS are addressing directly, still other problems that complicate an analyst's life in looking at non-U.S. countries will inevitably come under the IASC's purview.

■ *Consolidation.* What is included and what is not included in a consolidated statement? In the United States, a company must include every entity of which it owns more than 50 percent. That rule is not the case elsewhere. Companies have a lot of discretion as to what they include and exclude, particularly the decision about whether a subsidiary is, in fact, comparable to the rest of the entities a company is consolidating. Manufacturing companies, for example, tend to leave out finance subsidiaries. For years, although their practice is slowly changing, the Japanese have omitted those subsidiaries that are "not material." Those subsidiaries may not be material from the earnings point of view, but they can be highly leveraged.

An analyst who is examining financial statements of a non-U.S. company should first make sure that he or she is not looking at a parent company statement. Such statements are not presented in the United States but are common elsewhere. Next, the analyst needs to get a good understanding of what the consolidation rules are.

■ *Extraordinary items.* Another concern, although less so today than in the past, is extraordinary items. Outside of the United States, the rules governing extraordinary items were, for many years, very liberal. Whatever companies thought was extraordinary, they called extraordinary.

Fortunately, this practice has been increasingly restricted. In fact, in the United Kingdom today, extraordinary items are very rare. France, however, has expanded the list of possible extraordinary items, and practices still vary.

An analyst should always ask how these extraordinary items would be presented, say, under U.S. GAAP. They would probably be unusual items, not extraordinary, and they would probably be operating items.

■ *R&D costs.* R&D can be capitalized in many countries around the world. In fact, IAS encourage companies to capitalize development costs and even make it mandatory if a company believes those costs are recoverable. This practice may be economic reality, but most analysts would still say to expense these costs as incurred.

- *Depreciation.* A major accounting difference among countries is the treatment of depreciation, which in the United States also differs from company to company; relatively few companies use accelerated depreciation, and some use straight-line depreciation.

The difference overseas is that companies are using depreciation for tax purposes. Tax depreciation is book depreciation. Depreciation lives have very little to do with the economic lives of the assets and everything to do with government tax policies. Hence, depreciation lives tend to be shorter than economic lives.

Another problem in other countries is excess depreciation. A company has a little extra profit that is taxable, so it says, "Let's record some excess depreciation"—depreciation beyond what it would normally charge. Typically, excess depreciation is a tax decision.

- *Leases.* Outside the United States, leases tend to be treated as operating leases. The treatment of leases, however, has changed in some countries. Japan, for example, moved recently to a capital lease or financing type of lease accounting. The problem is that company managements still want to record operating leases, so most of the rules have been written to allow them to use an operating lease rather than having to capitalize a lease.

Analysts must look at leases very carefully. In fact, the group called the G4+1 (the representatives from the standard setters in Australia, Canada, the United Kingdom, and the United States plus the IASC) has become so frustrated with lease accounting abuse that it proposed to the group's constituent local rule-making bodies that leases that run for more then one year should be capitalized.

- *Pooling of interests.* In contrast to the many problems the U.S. SEC has encountered with pooling-of-interests accounting, pooling of interests is not a big problem elsewhere in the world. Outside the United States, companies can only use "uniting of interest" or merger accounting, which allows the pooling-of-interests method of accounting only when two companies come together with no clear acquirer. This rule limits the use of pooling accounting. In the United States, the FASB has just added a review of business combination accounting to its agenda. One result of this process, should the FASB move toward international standards and practices, might be that pooling-of-interests accounting could be practically eliminated in the United States in a few years.

## CONCLUSION

Today's IAS have taken a painfully long time to evolve, but the pace of developing new standards has picked up, and the acceptance of IAS is rapidly growing. In the meantime, the world and the way people do business is changing. Old standards must be interpreted in new circumstances. Evolution is inevitable. To meet this challenge, the IASC has set up a committee to keep IAS current with evolving business practices. As a result of this development and other IASC actions, I expect IAS to become more consistent with U.S. GAAP and to ensure greater consistency among countries, an obvious boon for U.S. investors.

In the future, as IAS are adopted, financial statements of non-U.S. companies will be more transparent. When Nestlé adopted IAS years ago, it had only a few accounting principle changes to make, but it had many new disclosure items to add in the form of notes. Thanks to IAS, corporate disclosures will certainly be more informative and more timely, especially for non-U.S. companies with U.S. listings.

Another development we will see is that companies will increasingly conform to all of the IAS. Recently, the IASC declared that if a company states it conforms to IAS, it must conform to *all* IAS. A declaration that the financial statement is in "substantial" conformity with IAS is no longer acceptable.

Is the world moving toward international accounting standards that better reflect economic reality? Based on the recent progress being made by the IASC and other rule-making bodies, and to the extent that investors and analysts value consistency, transparency, timeliness, and conformity, the answer to this question is a clear "yes."

# Question and Answer Session

## David F. Hawkins

**Question:** Will all corporations go to IAS? Will European companies now be subjected to reporting results on a shorter time horizon (e.g., quarterly)?

**Hawkins:** U.S. companies will not go to IAS; non-U.S.-listed companies will increasingly move to IAS. The IASC does not require that those companies go to quarterly reporting. Its position is that interim-reporting frequency requirements are a local option set by local regulators. Except for companies that list in the United States, you probably will not see quarterly reporting. Most countries will stick with six-month interim reports.

**Question:** What would you consider to be the characteristics of a superior-quality accounting standard?

**Hawkins:** I believe a superior standard is one that is so unambiguous that when companies apply it, they all apply it the same way. A superior standard is also one that reflects underlying economic realities, generates sensible and reasonably reliable results, and requires sufficient disclosure that analysts can understand the circumstances that surround a transaction. Finally, a superior standard should be readily auditable.

**Question:** Down the road, perhaps after there is a common European currency, do you see GAAP and IASC merging their principles into a common set of standards?

**Hawkins:** No. There always will be differences, such as the revaluation of fixed assets, which is permitted by IAS but not by U.S. GAAP.

**Question:** Do you expect new IAS to be adopted by U.S. companies (in lieu of U.S. GAAP) or only by those planning to issue stock on nondomestic exchanges?

**Hawkins:** The U.S. SEC will continue to require listed U.S. companies to use U.S. GAAP. U.S. companies will not want to have two sets of earnings numbers—one using U.S. GAAP and another using IAS—in the public domain. So, they will not use IAS for their foreign listings.

# Accounting for Business Combinations and Restructurings

Patricia A. McConnell
*Managing Director*
*Bear, Stearns & Company, Inc.*

> Every business day brings a seemingly endless stream of newly announced business combinations and restructurings. Determining the earnings and valuation consequences requires investors and analysts to address such key accounting issues as differences between the purchase and pooling methods and the specifics of restructuring charges.

Business combinations and restructurings, at first glance, seem to be unrelated, particularly from an accounting perspective. Restructurings often take place independently of a business combination scenario—companies changing their strategic plans, changing their direction and focus. A number of restructurings, however, take place prior to a business combination as companies try to make themselves attractive to a suitor; other restructurings take place subsequent to a business combination to fit the two businesses together. So, the two phenomena are indeed related. This presentation examines a variety of issues involved in accounting and reporting for business combinations and restructurings—from the criteria for a pooling of interests to the treatment of costs to exit a business activity.

## ACCOUNTING FOR BUSINESS COMBINATIONS

The investment and regulatory environment—Wall Street, regulators, the U.S. Department of Justice, and the government—is, and has been for some time, extraordinarily healthy for business combinations. Such combinations have been plentiful indeed, and most seem to be accounted for as poolings of interests.

### Criteria for Pooling-of-Interests Accounting

The following criteria for pooling of interests, as spelled out in Accounting Principles Board (APB) Opinion No. 16, have existed for almost 30 years:
1. Each company is autonomous and has not been a subsidiary or a division of another within two years.
2. Each company is independent and holds as intercorporate investments no more than 10 percent of outstanding voting common stock of the other.
3. The pooling of interests will be effected as a single transaction within 12 months.
4. Each company offers and issues only voting common stock for 90 percent or more of the target's voting common stock.
5. Neither company changes equity interest in voting common stock in contemplation of the combination within two years through
   - distributions to shareholders,
   - additional issuances,
   - exchanges, or
   - retirements of securities.
6. Each reacquires shares only for purposes other than business combinations. Treasury stock may preclude a pooling.
7. The ratio of interest of an individual common stockholder to those of other common stockholders in the combined entity remains the same.
8. Voting rights are retained and not restricted.
9. No contingent payments are allowed; consideration is resolved at the date the plan is consummated.
10. The combined company does not agree directly or indirectly to retire or reacquire all or part of the common stock issued to effect combination.
11. The combined corporation has no agreements for the benefit of former shareholders of the combining company, such as guaranty of a loan secured by the stock issued, which negates the exchange of equity securities.

12. The combined company does not plan to dispose of a significant part of the assets of the combined company within two years except in the ordinary course of business or to eliminate duplicate facilities.

The relative importance of various of these criteria changes as the business environment changes, and some are especially important in today's environment.

▪ *Criterion 4.* The fourth criterion, stating that the acquiring company offers and issues only its own voting common stock for at least 90 percent of the target's voting common stock, is central for pooling of interests. This critical condition goes to the underlying nature and heart of what a pooling of interests is supposed to represent. The underlying theory of pooling-of-interests accounting is that two shareholder groups are combining their interests in two separate companies and sharing equally the risks and rewards of those two companies. The way to achieve that end is for both shareholder groups to become shareholders of the combined enterprise, hence the language of this criterion.

▪ *Criterion 1.* The first criterion states that each company is autonomous and that neither has been a subsidiary or a division of another company within the past two years. In the current business environment, this condition frequently becomes an obstacle to pooling-of-interests accounting; some companies, for example, have been spun off to shareholders by their parent company in a tax-free transaction within the past two years. Thus, they have been a subsidiary of the parent company within the past two years. Other companies that were taken private by management or by financial investors in leveraged buyout transactions during the 1980s recently have been taken public. While those companies were private, they may be deemed to have been subsidiaries of venture capital firms. If, in turn, those venture capital investors were active rather than passive, the companies cannot engage in a pooling of interests until two years after the venture capital investor's interest has been reduced below 50 percent. Other companies are technically still subsidiaries of parent companies because they are owned more than 50 percent by those parent entities. Therefore, they are subsidiaries and would not be eligible to participate in a pooling, either as an acquirer or a target, until they have been independent companies for two years. This first criterion precludes companies in a wide variety of scenarios from the pooling alternative.

▪ *Criterion 2.* The second criterion requires that each company be independent of the other, that each hold an investment of no more than 10 percent of the voting common stock in the other company participating in the business combination. This criterion is increasingly important as more and more companies—particularly in the technological, biotechnological, medical, and pharmaceutical fields—form strategic alliances. In many of these alliances, the partners make equity investments in each other. Frequently, particularly in the high-tech and biotech areas, when a product that was being jointly developed comes to fruition, one of the alliance partners decides to buy out the other. In that situation, if the intercorporate investment was more than 10 percent—and it usually is closer to 20 percent—then the acquiring company is precluded from using pooling-of-interests accounting.

▪ *Criterion 12.* The 12th criterion states that the combined corporation does not plan to dispose of a significant part of the assets of the combined entity within two years, except in the ordinary course of business or to eliminate duplicate facilities. Thus, restructuring by the management of the combined entity becomes very difficult. It is impossible to participate in the kind of "buy-them-up, break-them-up" mentality that pervaded the 1980s. The U.S. SEC tends to interpret this particular criterion strictly.

The phrase "ordinary course of business" permits the combined company to sell inventory and to dispose of outdated or retired assets as it would in the ordinary course of business. The SEC, however, usually challenges the sale of duplicate facilities after a pooling of interests, and its staff frequently challenges management to demonstrate, with extensive documentation, that the facilities that are being disposed of were in fact genuinely duplicative. This criterion does not apply when the government makes the combined company dispose of assets for antitrust reasons; that is, pooled companies can undertake asset disposal within two years if so mandated by the government.

▪ *Criterion 6.* This criterion is the first of two rules covering stock buybacks. Prior to the business combination, each company can reacquire shares only for purposes other than a business combination; that is, treasury stock may preclude a pooling.

Enforcement of this criterion is spelled out in a lengthy SEC interpretation, the substance of which is that stock reacquired two years prior to the closing of the pooling generally will be considered "tainted." If that tainted treasury stock exceeds 10 percent of the shares that are going to be issued in the business combination, the combination has to be accounted for as a purchase rather than a pooling. The 10 percent exemption level is the inverse of the 90 percent voting stock requirement level cited in the fourth criterion. It follows that if 10 percent of the shares can be purchased for cash, then 10 percent of the transaction can be in treasury stock.

The tainted stock rules apply equally to what would be considered the acquirer and the target. Because of the nature of a pooling of interests, the accounting does not identify an acquirer and a target, so both are treated equally. In fact, if both the acquirer and the target have treasury stock, the treasury stock is combined for purposes of testing whether more than 10 percent of the shares being issued in the business combination would be tainted treasury stock.

The taint can be cured by reissuing those treasury shares before or simultaneously with the closing of the business combination. This cure has been used on a handful of occasions in the past few years, when the business combination would not otherwise have met this criterion because both the companies had been engaged in stock repurchase programs and enormous amounts of treasury stock were involved. Generally speaking, although reissue cures the taint and allows the pooling to go forward, the stock transaction is more dilutive from the perspective of the entire transaction. The combining company will be both issuing shares to the current holders of the target's stock and reissuing the treasury stock. If the treasury stock was at the target, the combining company will immediately exchange those shares for the shares of the acquirer. As a result, the combined business itself has even more shares outstanding than the ratio of exchange would imply.

■ *Criterion 10.* This criterion is the second of the two rules that cover stock buybacks. Subsequent to the business combination, the combined company cannot directly or indirectly retire or reacquire all or part of the common stock issued to effect the combination. This is a situation in which management and its auditors have sometimes pushed the limits of acceptable practice.

During the past 30 years, the SEC has typically questioned only buybacks that took place within six months following a pooling and that involved a large amount of stock. In general, if the company started buying stock back in reasonable amounts more than six months after the business combination, the SEC did not challenge it. In recent years, companies very obviously have been testing the limits of this particular approach. In situations in which investors did not like the dilution from the shares being issued in the anticipated *pro forma* results, management would simply tell those investors, "Don't worry; after six months, we will buy the stock back."

The SEC realized that stating the intention to buy back the stock violates the 10th criterion, and in early 1996, the SEC issued Staff Accounting Bulletin No. 96 formalizing its interpretation of this long-standing rule and reaffirming the rule's applicability. If any shares are reacquired during the six-month period following the closing of the business combination, the SEC automatically assumes that management had intended to buy those shares at the date the business combination closed. The number purchased is added to preexisting tainted shares and if the aggregate amount exceeds 10 percent of the shares in the business combination, purchase accounting will be required. For the period of six months to two years following the business combination, reacquiring stock should be no problem, provided there is no evidence that management intended to buy back stock during that period when the pooling closed.

With these rules in place and newly reaffirmed, stock buybacks have become very problematical. For instance, the SEC takes the view that an approved announced stock buyback program is prima facie evidence that management intends to buy back stock, because the SEC cannot distinguish whether that program, even if in existence for a period of time, was really in contemplation of a business combination. The SEC generally takes the position that the announced number of shares to be repurchased should be combined with the tainted shares in treasury. If the aggregate amount exceeds 10 percent, pooling of interests is precluded. Consequently, a number of companies, in anticipation of accounting for a business combination as a pooling of interests, have actually announced that they are terminating their stock buyback programs, which is probably unfortunate.

The SEC has taken its share of criticism about the stock buyback rules, but its motivations are simple and center on two issues. First, SEC rules are, in effect, regulations of the U.S. government, and the SEC is charged with upholding them. Second, the SEC has some concern that the stock buyback programs artificially support the stock price of the acquiring company and thus may prevent the target company shareholders from getting true fair value in the exchange. Apart from the facts that a premature buyback is a violation of the rules and the SEC must uphold the law, such a buyback may well not be fair to all participants in the business combination.

## Purchase versus Pooling

The APB Opinion No. 16 criteria are onerous, the SEC interprets them tightly, and they intrude into a company's management. They make it difficult to do restructurings, spin-offs, and stock buybacks. So, with all of these constraints, why do corporate managers try so hard to account for business combinations as poolings of interests? The answer lies in the pleasant cosmetic effects that result from pooling-of-interests accounting contrasted with purchase accounting.

The primary differences in the two accounting methods flow from their underlying nature. Theoretically, a pooling of interests occurs when two shareholder groups combine their interests in two enterprises and share the risks and rewards of those enterprises on an equal basis. All the accounting flows from that premise. When the two companies are combined in a pooling of interests, their balance sheets are simply added together at historical cost and their income statements are simply combined. The shares issued to the target's shareholders are not recorded at the fair value of those shares in the marketplace, and it is not the value the target's shareholders believe they are receiving; rather, those shares are recorded on the balance sheet at the book value per share of the target company.

In contrast, accountants view a purchase business combination as the acquisition of the net assets of the target. As in an acquisition of any basket of net assets, they account for the combination at the fair value of the consideration paid to acquire the assets. The fact that a company is acquiring a factory through the acquisition of another company's stock does not change how the accountants should record the cost of that factory; it is recorded at fair value. In a purchase business combination, the consideration given can be all cash or all stock or a combination of cash and securities. The consideration will be valued at fair value, however, and that fair value will be allocated to the basket of assets acquired. Both the tangible and the identifiable intangible assets will be recorded at their fair value. If the purchase price, the fair value of the consideration given, exceeds the fair value of those assets, goodwill will be recorded.

Writing up the assets to their fair value will affect the income statement. There will be additional depreciation, so the combined companies' depreciation will be greater than the sum of each separate company's depreciation, and the goodwill that was created will have to be amortized. U.S. accounting rules state that goodwill should be amortized over its benefit period, not to exceed 40 years. The SEC, through the registration and review process, has been restricting that period to a shorter and shorter time, resulting in an amortization period that is probably, on average, closer to 25 years in the aggregate for U.S. corporations. Nonetheless, the goodwill must be amortized, an additional charge to the combined companies' earnings. Thus, in a business combination accounted for as a purchase, except in unusual circumstances, the combined earnings of the two companies will be less than the sum of the target and the acquirer's earnings because of the additional depreciation resulting from the write-up of the assets and the amortization of the goodwill, not to mention the additional cost of goods sold from writing up the inventory. Contrast that result with a pooling of interests, wherein the combined companies' earnings will be exactly equal to the sum of the target and the acquirer's earnings.

The financial statement presentations of pooling and of purchase are very different, and the issue is whether that difference should matter to the combined companies' valuation. Do the numbers that the accountants write down in the books and that are reported change the value of the enterprise? **Table 1** illustrates the accounting differences and potential impact on the valuation of the combined enterprise. Two companies—Purchase Company and Pool Company—have identical balance sheets. They each have cash of $100, liabilities of $50, and equities of $50. They both have $20 of earnings before interest, taxes, depreciation, and amortization (EBITDA) and $10 of net income.

Target, the company to be acquired, has assets of $70, liabilities of $30, and equity of $40. Target's EBITDA is $15, and its net income is $4. The fair value of Target's fixed assets is $90, and those assets have a useful life of 10 years. Purchase and Pool both offer Target shareholders $125 market value in their own common stock in exchange for Target's common stock. Purchase, unfortunately, must account for the transaction as a purchase business combination, even though it is using 100 percent stock, because it violated APB No. 16. Pool, on the other hand, can use pooling-of-interests accounting. That is its reward for not having done stock buybacks, divestitures, or restructuring.

Table 1 contrasts the *pro forma* results that would occur if Purchase acquired Target to those that would occur if Pool acquired Target. Adding together the balance sheets of Pool and Target, the equity section of the combined company now reflects the original $50 of Pool's equity plus the $40 of Target's equity. In other words, the $125 worth of stock that was issued is recorded on Pool's balance sheet at only $40, Target's book value. Purchase has to do purchase accounting, so when it combines Target's assets with its assets, it does so at their fair value ($100 Purchase + $90 Target), and it has to record goodwill, which in this transaction is $65. The equity of the company that is doing purchase accounting has increased to $175, the sum of its original $50 equity and the $125 of stock that it issued, valued at fair value on the date of issue.

Although the balance sheets are substantially different, Purchase management perceives the real problem to be its income statement. As Table 1 shows, the EBITDA of the two companies combined is $35 for both Purchase and Pool, which is their original EBITDA of $20 plus Target's EBITDA of $15. From

### Table 1. Purchase versus Pooling: An Example

| Item | Purchase Company | Pool Company |
|---|---|---|
| Cash | $100 | $100 |
| Assets | 90 | 70 |
| Goodwill | 65 | 0 |
| Total assets | $255 | $170 |
| Liabilities | $80 | $80 |
| Equity | 175 | 90 |
| Total liabilities and equity | $255 | $170 |
| Income before taxes, depreciation, and amortization | $ 35 | $ 35 |
| Original depreciation of target's assets ($70 divided by 10 years) | (7) | (7) |
| Additional depreciation of target's assets ($20 divided by 10 years) | (2) | 0 |
| Goodwill amortization ($65 divided by 35 years) | (2) | 0 |
| Income before tax | $ 24 | $ 28 |
| Tax currently payable ($28 times 50 percent) | 14 | 14 |
| Net income | $ 10 | $ 14 |
| Add: | | |
| Depreciation | 9 | 7 |
| Amortization | 2 | 0 |
| Operating cash flow | $ 21 | $ 21 |
| Taxes | 14 | 14 |
| EBITDA | $ 35 | $ 35 |

*Source*: Bear, Stearns & Company.

that amount is subtracted the original depreciation of Target's assets. Purchase has an additional $2 of depreciation resulting from having recorded the assets acquired at their fair value. In addition, Purchase will have goodwill amortization of approximately $2 based on a 35-year period.

Pool's income before tax is $28, and Purchase's is $24. The tax currently payable, which will be the actual cash taxes that they have to pay, is $14 for both companies, their income after original depreciation ($28) times 50 percent (the assumed tax rate). This example assumes that Purchase did not get a tax deduction for the additional depreciation and goodwill. Because qualifying for the additional deduction is difficult under U.S. tax law, companies that use purchase accounting rarely get the deduction; also, companies that pool can never get the additional deduction. Thus, the after-tax income is $14 for Pool and $10 for Purchase. That outcome is what management finds so onerous about purchase accounting—that the combined net income after the acquisition is lower than the income resulting from pooling.

The third section of Table 1 illustrates the calculation of two additional performance measures that the investment community would likely apply to the Purchase and Pool statements—operating cash flow and a cash flow surrogate that is referred to as EBITDA. Adding depreciation and amortization to net income gives operating cash flow, and adding taxes to operating cash flow gives EBITDA. The cash flows and the EBITDA of Purchase and Pool are identical, even though their net incomes are very different. The troubling question is whether the companies will be valued differently in the marketplace.

Regulators and many managements perceive that the marketplace actually would and does value these two companies differently based on whether they use pooling or purchase accounting. Granted, Purchase's use of a different form of consideration might warrant a different valuation because Purchase might have a different cost of debt than of equity capital. Changing the form of consideration may, in fact, change the economics of a transaction. But assuming that the consideration and the economics are the same, the valuation of a company should not differ based on how it does the accounting for the combination. All else equal, the way the transaction is accounted for should have nothing whatsoever to do with a company's valuation. Yet, the perception is that every time the *Wall Street Journal* or *Barron's* reports a business combination that cannot be done as a pooling, the company's stock price goes down. Why is that? Aren't companies supposed to be valued on cash flow? Because these questions are open, companies often go to great lengths to avoid the unpleasant cosmetic results of increased depreciation, especially increased goodwill amortization that results from purchase accounting.

High-tech and biotech companies have been able to avoid the creation of goodwill without the use of pooling by writing off goodwill at the date of acquisition as "in-process R&D." FASB rules have long stated that research and development costs incurred in-house must be expensed; in response, many companies developed strategies for reciprocal purchases of R&D from each other and for capitalizing that R&D. Then, the FASB ruled that purchased R&D must be expensed, rather than capitalized, in the same fashion as in-house R&D. This rule, originally promulgated to stop a perceived abuse, is now very fortuitous for companies in the high-tech and biotech industries in which consolidation has become fashionable. Acquirers are paying huge sums for R&D, essentially, because no or few hard assets exist. Acquirers certainly do not want to attribute the cost to intangibles or to goodwill; that would drag the newly combined company's earnings down at the outset. Thus, companies are attributing more and more of the purchase price to acquired "in-process R&D," which must be expensed.

Not surprisingly, the SEC has engaged in a continuing effort to press such companies to place a realistic valuation on the in-process R&D, rather than merely treating it as a residual, and to value acquired R&D using the same measures as are applied to in-house R&D. The issues are still evolving, and analysts should exercise caution. In the software industry, for example, companies are allowed to capitalize the development costs of software that has reached technological feasibility. Some companies seem to define that point as crystallization of an idea; others define it to be when they ship the shrink-wrapped package. The spectrum of technological feasibility is obviously broad indeed. So, the struggle over accurate valuation is ongoing and clearly unresolved, but the larger point is that these companies, which are working so hard to "hide" goodwill and similar items, must perceive that the market does not look past the cosmetic differences imparted by the accounting method.

## ACCOUNTING FOR RESTRUCTURINGS

Yet another way companies try to improve their reported results subsequent to a business combination is through restructurings. The beneficial effects of restructuring charges are on the income statement, and companies continually search for ways to make the income statement effects of combinations palatable to investors.

### GAAP Income Statements

Table 2 represents the current state of the art in income statement presentation. In this income statement, the captions are defined by generally accepted accounting principles (GAAP). Revenue and expense are defined in GAAP terms; costs can be capitalized or expensed depending on whether they provide future benefits. Ironically, the first subtotal, revenue less expense, which users think of as operating income, and which is important to analysis, is not defined well anywhere in GAAP. The first subtotal that is defined in an accounting standard is income from continuing operations before income tax, discontinued operations, extraordinary items, and the cumulative effect of an accounting change; an "above the line" item usually is found before this subtotal. Subtracting provision for income taxes results in a second subtotal found in the GAAP literature, which is income from continuing operations before discontinued operations, extraordinary items, and the cumulative effect of an accounting change; a "below the line" item usually is found after this subtotal. For example, discontinued operations and extraordinary items are both below-the-line items.

■ *Discontinued operations.* To be considered "discontinued" under GAAP, an operation has to be a single, separate, major line of business and the company must be getting entirely out of that line of business or no longer serving that class of customer. To illustrate how this rule fits in with restructuring charges, consider a hypothetical example of a company that has three factories, two of which make running shoes and one of which makes athletic clothing. The company is going to restructure, and the board of directors is faced with three alternative scenarios for restructuring.

Scenario 1 is to shut down one of the running shoe factories. If it does that, it will not have a discontinued operation because it will still have a running shoe factory. Any gain or loss from that action would have to be shown above the line, pretax, and management would probably label that a restructuring charge—if not on the face of the income statement, certainly in the footnotes and in the management discussion and analysis (MD&A).

Scenario 2 is that the company leaves both running shoe factories open but closes its athletic clothing factory. Once it does that, it is out of the business of making athletic clothing. That closure would qualify as a discontinued operation, would be labeled as such, and could be shown below the line net of tax. Again, in the footnotes and in the MD&A, the company would probably refer to that amount as a restructuring charge.

Scenario 3 involves shutting down one running shoe factory *and* the athletic clothes factory. The company would have one charge that would be

### Table 2. GAAP Income Statement Presentation

| | |
|---|---:|
| Revenue | $XXXXX |
| Expense | XXXXX |
| | $ XXXX |
| Other revenue and expense | XXX |
| Income from continuing operations before income tax, discontinued operations, extraordinary items, and the cumulative effect of an accounting change | $ XXXX |
| Provision for income taxes | XXX |
| Income from continuing operations before discontinued operations, extraordinary items, and the cumulative effect of an accounting change | $ XXXX |
| Discontinued operations (note X): | |
| Income (loss) from operations of discontinued Division X (less applicable income taxes of $XXX) | $ XXXX |
| Loss on disposal of Division X, including provision of $XXX for operating losses during phase-out period (less applicable income taxes of $XXX) | XXXX |
| | $ XXXX |
| Extraordinary items (less applicable income taxes of $XX; note X) | $ XXX |
| Cumulative effect of an accounting change (less applicable income taxes of $XX; note X) | $ XXX |
| Net income | $ XXX |

*Source*: Bear, Stearns & Company.

above the line, pretax—shutting down the running shoe factory—because that does not qualify as a discontinued operation, and the company would have another charge for closing down the athletic clothing factory, a below-the-line, net-of-tax discontinued operation. The MD&A and the footnotes would probably lump the two charges together and refer to them as restructuring charges.

One of the reasons that analyzing these charges is so complex is that the three scenarios seem similar, yet one is above the line, pretax; one is below the line, net of tax; and one is both. Although these charges have different labels in the income statement, management, in discussing the charges, will more than likely combine them as restructuring charges.

■ *Extraordinary items.* Extraordinary items also go below the line, net of tax. To be extraordinary, an item must be unusual in nature and occur infrequently. These items are evaluated within the environment in which the company operates. For example, a company that has a factory in the middle of the desert that is destroyed by a flood could probably report that as an extraordinary item because it is very unusual in nature and it is infrequent. On the other hand, if that factory were on the banks of the Missouri River, the company could not call it an extraordinary item because the factory has probably been flooded before and it will probably be flooded again. Whether an item goes below the line and is characterized as extraordinary depends not so much on the event itself as on the environment in which the enterprise operates.

Arbitrary exceptions do exist, however. For instance, the most frequently cited extraordinary item is probably the gain or loss from early extinguishment of debt. Why should that be extraordinary? It does not meet the definition of extraordinary; rather, FASB rules, for whatever reason, simply require that treatment.

Restructuring charges per se do not appear anywhere in the income statement presented in Table 2. That is because a restructuring charge is not defined in GAAP. Management may refer to restructuring charges in the context of discontinued operations or extraordinary items or above-the-line items. Where do restructuring charges explicitly fit in the GAAP reporting scheme?

## The Specifics of Restructuring Charges

Restructuring charges will typically result from the consolidation and/or relocation of operations, the abandonment of operations or productive assets, and/or the impairment of productive assets. Some of these situations—for instance, abandonment of operations—might also qualify for treatment as discontinued operations.

A restructuring charge is usually composed of a write-down of fixed assets; a write-down of inventory; a write-off of patents and trademarks (which are all noncash items); and a provision for employee termination costs and perhaps relocation costs, which will both require the payment of cash.

Generally, the restructuring charge will be a component of income from continuing operations, and it will be separately disclosed if material. The only time such a charge will show up below the line is when it qualifies as a discontinued operation or an extraordinary item. The SEC will not allow companies to present this restructuring charge in a way that implies that some subtotal above the charge is income from continuing operations. The SEC contends that most restructuring charges must be included in income from continuing operations and prohibits using the caption "Income from continuing operations before restructuring charges."

Why would the SEC adopt this stance when these charges seem to be nonrecurring? The problem is that, because of their very nature, some of them may be recurring. A few years ago, the SEC investigated a number of restructuring charges that were taken by registrants. It found that many items being included in restructuring charges would not be considered, even by the most liberal of observers, nonrecurring.

As an example, assume a retailer acquired another retailer and did a restructuring. The acquiring retailer had an image to maintain, and part of the restructuring was to make the acquired retailer fit the image, which would obviously require removal of the old retailer's sign, clearly a restructuring charge. But then the acquirer had to put up the new sign, which it also expensed. The acquirer also had to redo the inside of the acquired store so that it had the same ambiance as the acquirer's. All the leasehold improvements of the acquired store had to be written off, which is legitimate, but all the new carpets and chandeliers and potted palms were also expensed. That treatment helped offset the amortization of the goodwill; that is, many leasehold improvements were not going to have to be amortized now because, having been expensed as restructuring charges, they no longer existed.

Companies were obviously pushing the envelope on what they characterized as restructuring charges, and as in the example, some companies expensed costs that most observers would consider to be assets, or expenditures that were going to benefit the company in the future. Based on these findings, the SEC brought several enforcement actions requiring companies to restate previously reported earnings.

## Employee Termination Benefits

Another problem the SEC found related to employee termination benefits. For instance, a company took a restructuring charge, the bulk of which was to be for downsizing. Upon investigation, the SEC found that the amount of the charge for employee termination benefits had no basis in fact. The company argued that it decided late in the fourth quarter to restructure and did not have time to do a formal analysis. The company merely guessed at what the termination was going to cost, and the guess was substantially too high; in fact, the company found out subsequently that no terminations were required. What did the company do with this reserve it had set up on its balance sheet for employee termination? The company simply reversed the charge back into earnings, increasing earnings per share. The company forgot to mention the reversal, however, in its MD&A or footnotes.

In response to these and similar abuses, the SEC took the issue of restructuring charges to the FASB's Emerging Issues Task Force (EITF), which has established some parameters for when an expense can be recorded and how it is measured.

The EITF concluded that before a company can take a restructuring charge and set up a reserve, or a liability, for employee terminations, it must have a specific plan for terminations. The company cannot merely say it needs to take a charge. Rather, it must have a plan that establishes the benefits that employees will receive if they are terminated; that identifies the number of employees to be terminated by class or function and location of employee; and that has been communicated to the employees. The thinking is that if management actually has a plan, has defined the benefits, has communicated that information to the employees, and has designated who is going to be terminated, the likelihood of the charge being real is high. At that point, the company can accrue the liability and take the charge.

Every time accountants make a rule, however, a problem turns up on the other side of the rule. The good parts of this rule are that it leads to restructuring charges that are much better estimates; the time frame for implementation is shorter; a company will be less likely to reverse a charge into earnings; and any such reversal must be disclosed in the footnotes. The downside is that some employee terminations result in a "dribble-through" effect on earnings if management is not ready to commit to a rigorous termination plan. Situations occur in which a company's management states that the selling, general, and administrative (SG&A) expense is going to be a bit high for the next several quarters because of downsizing but that the EITF rules are so strict that the company cannot take a one-time charge or a reserve. So, these expenses, management says, can only flow through SG&A as the employees walk out the door, a "bit" at a time. The question is: Does this management really have a termination plan.

## Costs to Exit an Activity

The EITF also addressed the recognition and measurement of other costs that go into restructuring charges—for example, writing down or writing off inventory and fixed assets. The EITF does not refer to these as restructuring charges but, rather, as costs to exit an activity that did not qualify as a discontinued operation. As in the case of employee termination, management cannot simply arbitrarily accrue a charge. The rules require that management have a plan that specifies the activities that will be discontinued and that addresses how management is going to dispose of those activities. Are the assets to be disposed of piecemeal or in their entirety? Are they being scrapped or salvaged? Management must identify the location of the activities that are being discontinued and the expected date of completion. The SEC wants this expected date of completion to be in the foreseeable future, certainly within the next five years but preferably within 18–24 months. In short, management must disclose the activities that are being discontinued, the method of disposition, the anticipated date of completion, and the type and amount of the costs recognized as a liability and expensed as a restructuring charge. A whole host of disclosures are now required about this component of a restructuring charge.

This information helps identify which portion of the restructuring charge will require cash and which part will not use cash, which portion is actually nonrecurring and which part might be overstated in order to bank future earnings. Distinguishing between recurring and nonrecurring charges is still difficult; write-downs of inventory and fixed assets offer two prime examples of the difficulty.

■ *Inventory write-down.* In the case discussed earlier in which one retailer acquires another retailer and must combine the corporate image and styles, a write-down of inventory would likely be involved. For instance, management might aggressively mark down some of the inventory that it acquired from the target so as to clear the shelves for new merchandise that fits its image. Perhaps the markdown would be 60 percent in order to sell the old merchandise. Is that write-down of a one-time nature? In the normal cycle of business, the acquirer might be marking down all of its goods by 40 percent anyway (because for example, it does not want to store bathing suits over the winter). How much of that restructuring charge, the write-down of inventory, then is actually because of restructuring and how much would have occurred anyway as a normal markdown to sell the seasonal inventory?

Sometimes that distinction is nearly impossible to make, and the SEC has encouraged the EITF to rule that a write-down of inventory cannot be lumped into and characterized as a restructuring charge. The lack of a specific definition for a restructuring charge, however, makes it difficult for the EITF to say a company cannot characterize a write-down as a restructuring. So, the SEC will frequently challenge that portion of the restructuring charge that is a write-down of inventory. The unresolved questions are these: Will the apparent margin improvement be as good as a write-down might indicate, or was an accrual made for an embedded, normal, recurring markdown?

■ *Fixed-asset write-down.* Another noncash charge that can be difficult to identify as nonrecurring results from a write-down of fixed assets to their net realizable value. Net realizable value is a very subjective number that is based on many assumptions. The historical rule of thumb is that fixed-asset write-downs cannot be conservative enough; the philosophy is: Let's write those assets down and get them off the balance sheet. When companies write assets down but keep using them, they generate revenue for which there are low or no depreciation costs, which artificially improves earnings.

When the company genuinely is not going to use assets, when it is going to dispose of them, if it writes those assets down to a level below their net realizable value, the disposal will actually result in a gain. Management has discretion to determine whether that gain is material enough to disclose, because materiality is not well defined in GAAP. Although the asset gain may not be material to the year as a whole, it may be material to the quarter or to the line item that contains the gain. For instance, claiming that the gain is immaterial for the year, management might include it in SG&A, which could improve margins in a material way.

## CONCLUSION

Accountants make rules, and most of the time, those rules are genuinely intended to provide useful information. They also are trying to record what happened, and analysts are trying to forecast what will happen. Those two objectives are not always synchronized. Financial statements are useful but are best approached with healthy skepticism, frequent questioning, and persistent analysis. These qualities are especially needed in assessing the real financial consequences of business combinations and restructurings.

# Question and Answer Session

Patricia A. McConnell

**Question:** Which method is best, pooling or purchasing? Does the market discriminate between the two methods?

**McConnell:** The answer to the first question is easy: It doesn't matter. The answer to the second question is hard: In fact, I wish I knew the answer; I would like to be able to present the FASB and the SEC with solid information that says the difference doesn't matter to the market, that the market values the companies on the economics of the transaction. Academic studies show that the market is not fooled. However, individual market participants (some company managers and some analysts) do not accept the studies and will point to individual, isolated situations to support their case. The problem is one of perception over reality. Much anecdotal evidence suggests that the market thinks the earnings are better for a pooling than for a purchase. The market may penalize the company that has large amounts of goodwill amortization but not its competitor that did just as many acquisitions but was able to do them as poolings.

In the long term, the issue will become moot because of the FASB's current project on business combinations; the FASB is likely to move to the world standard on business combinations, which says that the only time a company can use pooling-of-interests accounting is when the acquirer cannot be identified. That usually means the acquirer and target are of equal size. Although the FASB will probably not prohibit pooling entirely, the narrow circumstances set forth in the world standard will greatly reduce pooling-of-interests transactions.

**Question:** Is there a tax advantage for pooling versus purchase?

**McConnell:** A stock-for-stock exchange that is nontaxable to the shareholders until they sell the shares received sometimes makes the transaction easier or allows the price to be lower because it is a nontaxable transaction to the shareholder. If the exchange were taxable to the shareholders, they might have to pay a higher premium for the target company. A stock-for-stock exchange does not necessarily preclude doing purchase accounting; the same tax advantage is available in a purchase business combination by using stock for the consideration.

Goodwill is another potential tax-related issue. Until 1993, goodwill was not tax deductible in the United States. Since 1993, in limited circumstances, goodwill is tax deductible, but in fact, the rule that permits goodwill to be amortized for tax purposes is almost never invoked in a public market transaction. So, the sum and substance of the tax question is that purchase and pooling can have similar tax consequences.

**Question:** How long can a company be carried as a discontinued operation?

**McConnell:** APB No. 30, which defines a discontinued operation, clearly states that the discontinuance must be completed within one year. For a long time, either nobody read this rule or they simply ignored it, but recently, the SEC began enforcing it. The SEC has required companies to restate earnings if an operation was classified as discontinued for more than a year before it was disposed of. The SEC has tried to apply that same notion, that the time period for restructuring has to be very short, to restructuring charges. This application certainly complicates a company's decision making and the analyst's job. Management may want to sell an operation but does not think it can do it within the year, so it cannot classify the operation as discontinued. Thus, the company could well have an operation that is publicly and visibly for sale but that is not being carried as discontinued. For forecasting purposes, analysts would like to see the operation classified as discontinued at the earliest opportunity. So, the SEC's enforcement in this area does create some unforeseen difficulties for financial statement analysis.

**Question:** Should analysts add back or ignore restructuring charges?

**McConnell:** A blanket approach is inappropriate. The answer depends on the facts and circumstances of the situation. For instance, suppose a company has taken a restructuring charge, a write-down of fixed assets. Is that write-down entirely or partly because the company underdepreciated the assets in the past? If so, that charge should be taken back to prior earnings to get a different sort of, and more accurate, earnings trend. Or is it actually a one-time event? Did technology change in the industry? Is it something that the company cannot control that means it has to get rid of certain equipment and put in all new equipment? That would probably be a one-time event, something that the company could not control. So, the approach is on a "facts and circumstances" basis. When the items are legitimately one time and nonrecurring, the analyst can take them out of earnings, but only after careful evaluation.

**Question:** Do you believe there will be a crackdown on technology companies' use of in-process R&D write-downs? If so, what kind of companies might be hurt?

**McConnell:** I believe the FASB, in its project on accounting for business combinations, is going to review the current rule requiring the write-off of in-process R&D. In theory, it should not hurt anyone. Accountants cannot create value, and they cannot take it away.

**Question:** What rules govern write-downs of long-lived assets, particularly goodwill on continuing operations?

**McConnell:** Financial Accounting Statement (FAS) No. 121 is the accounting standard covering a write-down of long-lived assets, including goodwill. Under FAS No. 121, when an impairment is indicated, management must group the potentially impaired assets, including goodwill, at the lowest level for which cash flows can be identified. Management then aggregates its forecast of future cash flows from these assets. If cash flows equal or exceed the carrying amount of the assets, there is no impairment. If the aggregate forecasted cash flows are less than the carrying amount, then management is to measure the write-down by the difference between the assets' earnings amount and the *discounted* present value of the forecasted cash flows. This impairment loss is applied first to any goodwill included in the asset group being treated for impairment.

**Question:** What are the guidelines on disclosure of reversal of reserves and gain on sale of written-down assets? Can it be spread over multiple periods and transferred to other reserves?

**McConnell:** Because a restructuring reserve is an estimate, it should be assessed for reasonableness each period. So, it might be increased or decreased quarterly as circumstances change. The increase or decrease will run through income and be disclosed in a footnote if deemed material.

**Question:** How is "significant part" of assets defined in Criterion 12?

**McConnell:** The SEC staff generally interprets assets to be a "significant part" of the combined companies' assets if they represent more than 10 percent of combined assets, revenues, or profits.

**Question:** Postpooling, what philosophy dictates the arbitrary two-year ban on buybacks other than "This is the rule"? Why is this rule different from any other capital-spending decision?

**McConnell:** The two-year time frame before and after a transaction is arbitrary. Stock buybacks are banned because they violate the underlying theory that supports the pooling-of-interest exception to recording assets acquired at cost. The justification for pooling is that it is not an acquisition of assets—in fact, it is not a transaction at all but merely the coming together of two shareholder groups to run their individual businesses as if they were one. If shares are repurchased by the acquirer or target either before or after the combination, then two shareholder groups are not coming together. Some of the shareholders have sold their shares and are no longer part of the group, which violates the underlying theory.

# The Effect of Taxes on Reported Earnings

Robert Willens
*Managing Director and Tax Analyst*
*Lehman Brothers*

> Taxes are an undeniable feature of whatever reality exists in reported earnings. An analyst faces three particularly important issues in assessing the effects of taxes on reported earnings: analyzing differences between accounting and taxable income, accounting for income taxes, and accounting for corporate capital trasactions.

Whatever constitutes the reality of reported earnings, taxes are an undeniable feature of that reality. Investors and analysts who ignore the contribution of taxes to the gap between economic and reported earnings do so at their own peril. This presentation details the effects of taxes on reported earnings, focusing particularly on three tasks critical to the analyst's work: analyzing differences between accounting and taxable income, accounting for income taxes, and accounting for corporate capital transactions.

## ACCOUNTING INCOME VERSUS TAXABLE INCOME

An important part of every corporate income tax return (Form 1120) filed with the Internal Revenue Service (IRS) is a completed Schedule M-1, which reconciles accounting net income to taxable income. The process of arriving at taxable income involves two steps: (1) adding back to after-tax accounting net income certain items that are not deductible for tax purposes but are deductible for accounting purposes and (2) subtracting items that are deductible for tax purposes but are not deductible for accounting purposes.

### Add-Back Items

Because of the differing objectives of tax accounting and financial accounting, Congress has decided that not every expenditure is properly deductible for tax purposes. In many cases, the selection of nondeductible items is arbitrary and identifying such items requires a knowledge of the tax law pertaining to them.

■ *Federal income taxes.* Federal income taxes are added back because the tax provision for accounting purposes is not a deduction item for tax.

■ *Net capital losses.* Any net capital losses are added back. For tax purposes, a corporation is permitted to deduct capital losses only to the extent that it has capital gains. Any excess capital losses or net capital losses can be carried back three years to recover taxes paid in prior years. If they are not fully absorbed in the carryback period, they are then carried forward for an additional five years. If a corporation sustains a capital loss in excess of its capital gains, it has eight years to use those losses.

The Quaker Oats Company may soon provide an illustration of this concept; many observers think Quaker will "cash in" what would probably amount to $1 billion in capital loss related to its Snapple Beverages business. Quaker has had capital gains in prior years from selling other businesses. Using the Snapple loss to recover the taxes paid on prior capital gains would make economic sense.

■ *Income items.* Various income items that are included for tax purposes but not for accounting purposes must be added back. For instance, advanced payments for goods and services are deferred for accounting purposes until the relevant services are rendered or the goods are delivered; for tax purposes, however, actual receipt of the money renders the payment taxable even though the services or goods have not been delivered.

■ *Capital contributions.* Some types of capital contributions are added back to accounting net income. Certain receipts are characterized as capital contributions for accounting purposes but constitute income for tax purposes—for example, when a governmental body makes payments to a corporation to induce it to relocate its facilities. Another example is the gain component of the current installment from an installment sale. For accounting purposes, the gain from an installment sale is recorded in the year in which the sale occurs; for tax purposes, the gain from property sold through the installment method (i.e., notes of the buyer) is reported when, as, and if the installment payments are actually received.

■ *Deductions.* Deductions that are taken for accounting purposes but are not eligible deductions for tax purposes must also be added back. One such item is restructuring charges. For tax purposes, the items that compose a restructuring charge are not deductible until they are paid, and a reserve or a restructuring provision is permitted only in certain specialized industries, such as insurance and banking. As a general rule, such items as these are deductible for tax purposes only when resources are actually expended with respect to those items. Another nondeductible item for tax purposes is expenses and interest incurred in earning tax-exempt interest income from municipal bonds; the income that those expenses produce is not taxable, so the expenses should be nondeductible.

## Subtractable Items

Adding back all these items results in a taxable income subtotal, which in turn, requires a final set of adjustments to arrive at taxable income. Specifically, from that subtotal are subtracted items that are deductible for tax purposes but are not deductible for accounting purposes.

■ *Dividends-received deduction.* The tax law has long provided for a dividends-received deduction, whereby a domestic corporation is entitled to a deduction for dividends received from another domestic corporation; the objective is to mitigate the effects of double taxation on corporate earnings. That deduction is unique to the tax law; it is not taken for accounting purposes, so it becomes a reconciling item on Schedule M-1.

Currently, the dividends-received deduction is 70 percent, so a corporate recipient of a dividend is entitled to deduct 70 percent of the amount of the dividend from its taxable income. If the recipient of the dividend owns at least 20 percent of both the voting power and value of the stock of the paying entity, the dividends-received deduction percentage is 80 percent. This provision is known as the "Seagram Rule." When the law was changed in 1987 to reduce the percentage to 70 percent, The Seagram Company owned 24 percent of DuPont and most of its earnings were derived from DuPont dividends. So, Seagram persuaded some of the senators to add this enhanced dividends-received deduction for situations in which the dividend-paying company is 20 percent owned by the dividend-receiving company.

■ *Excess depreciation.* Another tax deduction to be subtracted on Schedule M-1 is the excess of accelerated depreciation taken for tax purposes under the modified accelerated cost recovery system (MACRS), a double-declining balance system that provides relatively brief recovery periods for depreciable property. Here "excess" is defined to be the depreciation provided by MACRS over the depreciation that would be provided by straight-line depreciation, which is the method typically chosen for accounting purposes.

■ *Income items.* The final step in arriving at taxable income is to subtract income items that are recognized for accounting purposes but are not taxable. Common items are interest on municipal bonds and the proceeds from life insurance policies. Under Section 101 of the U.S. tax code, these proceeds are excluded from taxable income but are clearly part of book income. Also subtracted are gains on installment sales; the installment sale gain realized in the year the sale originates is an accounting income item, but the gain associated with the installment sale is deferred for tax purposes until it is recognized in the year or years the payments are made on the installment obligation. At that point, the seller multiplies the payment by the gross profit percentage calculated at the inception of the sale to determine the taxable portion of the installment sale.

Subtracting all these items from the previously determined taxable income subtotal results in the goal of Schedule M-1, a taxable net income figure that is reconciled with accounting net income.

## ACCOUNTING FOR INCOME TAXES

SFAS 109 deals with accounting for income taxes. Of particular interest to analysts, because of the potential for manipulation and lack of comparability, are the treatment of deductible temporary differences, the recognition of deferred tax assets, and the use of net operating losses (NOLs) in an acquisition context.

■ *Deductible temporary differences.* Management and auditors have much discretion in reporting restructuring charges. In the accounting world, a restructuring charge is typically not deductible for tax purposes when the charge arises but is deferred until the items that constitute the charge are actually paid or incurred. For tax purposes, a restructuring charge creates a temporary difference between accounting income and taxable income. This discrepancy is known as a deductible temporary difference—deductible in the sense that it has the potential to create a future tax benefit.

■ *Deferred tax assets.* A company can operate at a loss for a sustained period. If those operating losses are added to the deductible temporary differences that a company possesses and the sum is multiplied by the tax rate, the result is a gross deferred tax asset.

That gross deferred tax asset will presumably provide a benefit on the profit and loss (P&L) statement at some future point. Conceivably, that benefit will be generated in the year the gross deferred tax asset arises. Although this circumstance is entirely possible, it is not common because once the gross deferred tax asset is identified, the company's management and auditors must ascertain whether the future benefits associated with this gross deferred tax asset are "more likely than not" to be realized. The most common case is that the decision makers determine that the future benefits more likely will not be realized; perhaps, for instance, management is not sufficiently confident that the corporation will generate enough taxable income to use these operating losses. Then, the P&L benefit claimed must be deferred through the mechanism of a valuation allowance. That mechanism begins with the company recognizing a gross deferred tax asset. Upon concluding that the benefits of that asset are not likely to be realized, the company takes a reserve against the asset in the form of a valuation allowance. The object is to arrive at a net deferred tax asset, a number that is "more likely than not" to be realized.

Invariably, the companies that have generated these potential assets are companies that have a history of operating losses. For purposes of SFAS 109, that history is considered negative evidence with respect to the likelihood that the deferred tax asset will be realized. Significant negative evidence will require a full or substantially full valuation allowance. In essence, the entire amount of the deferred tax asset must be reserved. Once the losses have been stanched, the company hopes to enter into a period of sustained profitability. Until sustained profitability is achieved, however, the benefit of the deferred tax asset is limited annually to an amount sufficient to offset the current income tax charge. The company will draw down the deferred tax asset only in an amount necessary to offset the current income tax charge, to zero out its current tax provision.

If that period of profitability persists, however, management's judgment will become paramount again because the remaining balance of the deferred tax asset is then eligible to be drawn down beyond an amount sufficient to offset the current income tax charge. Once the company has crossed into the world of positive evidence in terms of the "realizability" of the deferred tax asset, then management has great discretion in drawing down that deferred tax asset. To the extent that it does draw down the deferred tax asset through the mechanism of reducing its valuation allowance, the company will realize an incremental P&L benefit equal to the amount by which the valuation allowance has been reduced.

Analysts should proceed with caution here; often in such situations, management, needing to hit ambitious earnings targets in a given period, uses the now-positive income stream to argue to the auditors that there is no longer a need for as much of a valuation allowance as before. If the auditors are convinced, the reduction in valuation allowance from period to period goes right to the P&L's bottom line; the company realizes a direct and dollar-for-dollar incremental P&L benefit that is accounted for through the tax provision.

Thus, the valuation allowance is a judgmental item that is susceptible to manipulation, and analysts should watch carefully for changes in the allowance; management should be questioned carefully about the appropriateness of drawing down the allowance.

■ *NOLs.* Questions frequently arise about when and how a company can use an NOL in an acquisition context. Congress has been very suspicious of companies with NOLs that are involved in the acquisition process, so suspicious about these transactions that it has labeled the process by which one corporation acquires another corporation with NOLs as "trafficking in NOLs." Thus, the tax rules, primarily found in Section 382 of the U.S. tax code, severely inhibit this use of NOLs, lessening the realizability of the deferred tax asset and directly increasing the magnitude of the valuation allowance.

If a company with NOLs experiences an ownership change, that company's ability to use its NOLs to offset taxable income subsequent to the ownership change is severely limited and how much income the NOLs can offset is determined somewhat counterintuitively. The value of the company's equity at the time of the ownership change is multiplied by the long-term tax-exempt rate, which is a composite yield on high-grade municipal bonds that is published monthly (in a press release) by the IRS to obtain what is known as the Section 382 limitation. This limitation measures the annual amount of taxable income that can be offset by a company's NOL carryforward subsequent to an ownership change.

For example, on October 31, 1995, Navistar International Corporation had $2 billion of NOLs; suppose its market cap was $800 million and the long-term tax-exempt rate was 6 percent. If Navistar were acquired, its Section 382 limitation would be $800 million times 6 percent, or $48 million. Thus, the annual amount of income that its NOL carryovers could offset would only be $48 million. But Navistar has NOLs of $2 billion, and NOLs have only a 15-year life for tax purposes. The $48 million annually for 15 years is $720 million. So, if Navistar were to experience an ownership change, ignoring present value calculations, 35 percent of its NOL could be used, but only spread over 15 years, and 65 percent of its NOL would disappear immediately. Thus, acquiring a company with substantial NOLs and using those NOLs in any extensive way is anything but a simple, or lucrative, proposition.

Ironically, the tax law has always been markedly more liberal in cases in which the loss company is the acquirer rather than the target. For example, at one time, Westinghouse Electric Corporation had huge NOLs, now used down to about $1.5 billion. When Westinghouse acquired CBS, the tax law placed virtually no restrictions on Westinghouse's ability to use its NOLs to offset CBS's income. The only type of CBS income that Westinghouse's NOLs could not offset were recognized built-in gains (gains from the sale of assets that are recognized within five years of an acquisition of a company with built-in gains, such as CBS, by a company such as Westinghouse that has built-in losses). Had Westinghouse sought to have CBS sell off assets at a profit within five years from the day Westinghouse acquired CBS, the gains from those sales could not be absorbed by Westinghouse's NOLs. Any other type of CBS income, including operating income, could, was, and will be offset by Westinghouse's NOLs without restriction. Moreover, there is no limit on Westinghouse's own ability to absorb with its NOLs its own built-in gains from sales of its assets.

The differential treatment of buyers and targets is not new; the law has always been asymmetrical in situations in which a loss corporation is acquired. When trafficking in NOLs, the amount of NOL that can be used annually following an ownership change is severely restricted. If the NOL company is the buyer, its ability to use its NOLs is virtually unrestricted. Therefore, companies with huge amounts of NOLs are always, from a tax viewpoint, much better acquirers than they are targets.

## ACCOUNTING FOR CORPORATE CAPITAL TRANSACTIONS

The variety and complexity of corporate capital transactions necessarily make for similarly varied and complex accounting rules and tax treatments. Analysts and investors see many such capital transactions, ranging from "splitoffs" and subsidiary mergers to "earnouts." Of particular interest are the implications of four acquisition-related issues: purchase accounting, "in-process" R&D, "recap" accounting, and a single-entity view of consolidation.

### Purchase Accounting

In purchase accounting, the accounting book value of the assets of the target company is revalued and stepped up at the time of the acquisition. That same step-up, however, is rare for tax purposes. To get a basis step-up for tax purposes comparable to the basis step-up that is mandated by the purchase accounting rules, the acquiring company has to make an affirmative election, known as a Section 338 election. A Section 338 election can only be made in the case of a qualified stock purchase—a purchase by one corporation of at least 80 percent of the stock of another corporation within a 12-month period. The 338 election is to step up the basis of the target's assets for tax purposes to reflect the price paid for its stock.

Why would a company choose not to make the 338 election? For tax purposes, it seems a company would always want a higher asset basis and higher depreciation and amortization charges. The problem is that the cost of making the 338 election has been prohibitively high since the 1986 tax law change.

For example, if the Clorox Company, in the process of buying Armor All, wants to make a 338 election, Armor All is treated as if it sold all of its assets on the day that Clorox acquired at least 80 percent of its stock. That is, Armor All is treated as though it sold all of its assets in a single transaction for an amount equal to their fair market value. Armor All is then treated as a new corporation that purchased the assets sold by the old corporation. The assets are viewed as having been purchased for an amount exactly equal to the amount for which they were sold. This mechanism is how the 338 election accomplishes the basis step-up in the target's assets. The problem is the deemed sale (the hypothetical sale from old company to new company), which provides the basis step-up.

Prior to the 1986 tax law change, Armor All did not have to recognize a taxable gain on that hypothetical sale. Instead, the deemed sale was largely nontaxable, so Clorox was able to get a tax-free basis step-up in the assets of Armor All. Since January 1, 1987, the hypothetical sale just described, which provides the mechanism for achieving the basis step-up, has been a fully taxable transaction. Now, the tax cost of the deemed sale greatly outweighs the present value of the tax savings to be enjoyed from stepping up the basis of the target's assets. Thus, companies do not make Section 338 elections, and the basis of the assets of a target company is not stepped up to current value for tax purposes.

The accounting result in the case in which no basis step-up for tax purposes is available could be interesting. All things being equal, the pretax income of the parent–target combination is reduced because the assets have been written up for accounting purposes. Consequently, depreciation and amortization charges will be higher, and the pretax accounting income would be reduced following a purchase accounting transaction. The company's tax liability should remain the same because the assets have not been written up for tax purposes. If all of those taxes, which have not changed, are charged to operations in the year they are incurred, then the company's net income will look bad and its effective tax rate will look high; the level of tax liability is unchanged, but the level of pretax income is depressed because of the basis step-up that purchase accounting entails.

Not all of those taxes, however, are in fact charged to operations. The company only charges to operations the taxes it would have incurred had it taken a Section 338 basis step-up for tax purposes. The taxes that are paid over and above that amount, because there is no basis step-up, are charged to a deferred tax liability reserve, which is offset by an equal debit to goodwill. Thus, those extra taxes will be charged to operations over an extended period of time, mimicking the amortization of the goodwill that was created in the acquisition.

## "In-Process" Research and Development

If buyer P's cost for target T exceeds the fair value of T's assets, the excess is goodwill that must be amortized over periods not exceeding 40 years. Companies use a variety of tactics and techniques to minimize the goodwill that would otherwise have to arise in a purchase accounting transaction. For example, to the extent that T's assets consist of assets used in an R&D project "in process," P is required to immediately write off the amounts allocated to those items. The rationale for this seemingly counterintuitive treatment is to equate the accounting for purchased R&D with the accounting for incurred or internal R&D, which is written off as it is incurred.

Not surprisingly, companies work hard to ascribe as much of the purchase price to this item as possible; every dollar ascribed to in-process R&D is a dollar less of goodwill to be amortized over an extended period. This method has been a tremendous benefit in many transactions in the high-tech, biotech, and computer-related industries. As this tactic becomes more well known, it will undoubtedly attract increasing scrutiny from the SEC and the Financial Accounting Standards Board (FASB). For now, when preparing *pro forma* statements in a merger and acquisition transaction, to be able to show that 82 percent of the purchase price will be written off immediately is obviously very helpful.

## "Recap" Accounting

Recap accounting, used primarily by people involved in leveraged buyouts (LBOs), is an obscure but relatively simple acquisition-related reporting technique. From the accounting viewpoint, recap accounting avoids "push-down" accounting, the situation in which P's new purchase price for T's stock is pushed down to T's separate financial statements; that is, the purchase accounting adjustments are pushed down from P's financial statements to T's. From the acquisition viewpoint, recap accounting reduces or eliminates undesirable earnings effects.

In a typical LBO that illustrates the use of recap accounting, Kohlberg Kravis Roberts & Company (KKR) recently took Bruno's private, investing money as the LBO sponsor in Bruno's in exchange for primary equity. At the same time, Bruno's borrowed a substantial amount of money, then used the equity capital and the debt capital it had just raised to redeem or repurchase 87 percent of its stock. The LBO buyer was careful to leave the existing shareholders with a significant continuing common equity interest in the company. Even though control of the target company has clearly changed, if the deal is structured so that the shareholders continue to own a significant stake in the target's common equity, the company is eligible for recap accounting. Purchase accounting does not apply; therefore, the book value of Bruno's assets does not change and no earnings effect results. Instead, its accounting net worth changes to reflect the increase from the new equity invested by KKR and the decrease from the amounts paid out in redemption.

LBO sponsors like recap accounting because the target's earnings are not penalized by the need to amortize purchase accounting adjustments. The company's target net worth may be and usually is severely reduced, but who cares about net worth? Earnings are the key. KKR is not avoiding goodwill but, rather, is avoiding the necessity of pushing down the goodwill to Bruno's books, in which earnings would be penalized. KKR is doing this as part of its larger strategy to eventually take Bruno's public with the best possible earnings picture, a picture not deflated by the need to amortize goodwill, as would be required by purchase accounting.

Realistically, this technique can be used only by a private buyer. General Motors Corporation cannot use recap accounting when it buys a company and leaves a minority interest outstanding, and it also cannot avoid the purchase accounting adjustments. Why not? Because if one of the target's new shareholders is such an entity as GM that owns sufficient stock to use either the equity method of accounting or consolidation, then that shareholder has to use purchase accounting in preparing its consolidated statements and it has to amortize the goodwill arising out of the acquisition. Thus, recap accounting is only usable when the acquiring entity does not care what its financial statements look like, as is the case with

KKR and other private buyers but is not the case with nearly all publicly held buyers.

## A "Single-Entity" View of Consolidation

The FASB's initiatives in corporate consolidation policy will, when adopted (possibly in 1997), result in dramatic changes in accounting for acquisitions. Essentially, parent companies and controlled subsidiaries will be viewed as a single entity; transactions involving parent companies acquiring the balance of, or selling off pieces of, controlled subsidiaries will become balance sheet transactions for the parent, not P&L items.

Under current practice, a parent company, P, owning 51 percent of a subsidiary company, S, and subsequently acquiring the balance of S would have to use purchase accounting and meet all the other requirements with respect to the acquisition of that minority stake. The FASB consolidation proposal adopts a new conceptual framework for viewing a consolidated group, a framework that suggests that a parent and a controlled subsidiary will be viewed together as a single entity. Therefore, if P buys in the minority interest in S, and P and S are viewed as a single entity, that transaction is nothing more than a distribution to owners. In fact, the payment will be accounted for as a treasury stock transaction. Presumably, P will have an accounting incentive to buy in the balance of S because it will not have to apply purchase accounting precepts in accounting for that acquisition. Instead, the premium that would otherwise be charged to goodwill will be charged to shareholders' equity as a treasury stock transaction. As was the case in recap accounting, however, the balance sheet effects are largely irrelevant; earnings are the key and, in this single-entity concept, buying in a minority interest will not penalize earnings.

The FASB consolidation approach would have a similar effect on parent companies that sell equity pieces of their subsidiaries. Under current practice, Staff Accounting Bulletin (SAB) 51 and SAB 84, if P controls S and S issues additional shares, P is allowed to record a gain if the per share offering price of the shares issued by S exceeds the carrying amount per share of those shares and the transaction is not part of a broader corporate reorganization.

Through the years, many companies have made heavy use of that technique. For example, Waste Management used to do many equity "carve-outs" of subsidiaries and was able to record gains in cases in which, as was inevitable, the offering price per share of the subsidiary stock exceeded the carrying amount of the share. This ability to book gains in these circumstances would also be interdicted by the FASB single-entity proposal. On the theory that the parent and the subsidiary are a single entity, the transaction would be accounted for as a treasury stock transaction and labeled as an investment by the owner.

## CONCLUSION

The payment of taxes obviously affects economic earnings; the question is the extent to which the accounting for various tax issues enables or hinders translating that economic reality into reported earnings. That question is an open one, but a critical first step is understanding the tax influences most amenable to manipulation and obfuscation—for instance, how accounting and taxable earnings are reconciled, and the earnings effects of the accounting treatment for income taxes and for corporate capital transactions. Tax returns and schedules, accounting rules and pronouncements, and agency regulations become the tools of analysts who would pursue that understanding.

# Question and Answer Session

## Robert Willens

**Question:** Is a company's Schedule M-1 publicly available?

**Willens:** You have to ask the companies. It is part of their tax return, which is not public information. You do not really need the Schedule M-1, however, because virtually all of the information is in either the tax footnote or the company's deferred tax liabilities, deferred tax assets, and rate reconciliation data. The items that are part of Schedule M-1 that constitute temporary differences for accounting purposes are contained in the latter, and the Schedule M-1 items that pertain to permanent differences (e.g., tax-exempt interest) are embodied in the tax footnote that reconciles the statutory rate to the actual rate.

**Question:** What tax law changes do you anticipate that would affect corporate earnings?

**Willens:** First, I do not expect any changes in the tax rates. I am concerned about a change that will not affect corporate earnings as much as it will impede corporate capital transactions: the likely elimination of what is termed the Morris Trust technique. A Morris Trust transaction is used when one corporation wants to acquire only part of the business of another corporation. The Boeing Company, for example, is acquiring Rockwell International Corporation's defense activity through a Morris Trust transaction. Rockwell will spin off all of its assets, other than its defense activity, into a company, and distribute the stock of that new company to its shareholders in what would amount to a tax-free spin off. Then, Boeing acquires old Rockwell, which contains only the defense business, in exchange for Boeing stock in a second-stage tax-free transaction. So, there are two tax-free transactions: the tax-free spin-off and the tax-free acquisition. This method is a very popular way of breaking up a company on a tax-free basis.

In March 1996, the Clinton Administration proposed a new rule that would all but eliminate the utility of Morris Trust transactions, and I expect the administration to reintroduce that rule in the fiscal 1998 budget. In anticipation of that possible change, many Morris Trust transactions will be announced in the near future.

**Question:** Why all the trouble to avoid goodwill, a noncash expense?

**Willens:** Quite simply because analysts and other observers still pay strict attention to reported earnings, not cash flow.

# Self-Evaluation Examination

1. Brownlee reports that the statistical association between earnings and stock returns has been historically:
   a. Strong and directly related to business volatility.
   b. Weak and directly related to business volatility.
   c. Strong and inversely related to business volatility.
   d. Weak and inversely related to business volatility.

2. Information about a company's strategy, opportunities, risks, and uncertainties would be included in what Brownlee terms:
   a. Segment reporting.
   b. Business reporting.
   c. Permanent earnings reporting.
   d. Open reporting.

3. Fridson argues that the purpose of financial reporting is to:
   a. Let observers know how the company is doing.
   b. Provide investors with useful information.
   c. Enable companies to obtain cheap capital.
   d. Reconcile economic and reported earnings.

4. Fridson uses which of the following examples to illustrate the power of underlying accounting assumptions:
   I. Recognizing a sale.
   II. Stretching depreciable life.
   III. Booking earnings advances.
   a. I only.
   b. I and II only.
   c. II and III only.
   d. I, II, and III.

5. Fridson argues that most financial reporting gimmicks are detected by which of the following types of ratios?
   a. Working capital.
   b. Leverage.
   c. Profit margins.
   d. Economic value added.

6. According to Staley, the most frequent sources of earnings manipulation include all of the following *except*:
   a. Depreciation.
   b. Nonrecurring revenues.
   c. Allowance for doubtful accounts.
   d. Gross revenues.

7. Staley uses all of the following as examples of manipulating selling, general, and administrative expense *except*:
   a. Booking a gain on sale of asset components in management services.
   b. Lengthening the period for bankruptcy charge-offs.
   c. Writing off past expenses.
   d. Failing to mark securities to market.

8. Staley identifies which of the following tasks as essential components of portfolio maintenance:
   I. Studying 10-K and 10-Q reports.
   II. Contacting management.
   III. Monitoring interim announcements.
   a. I only.
   b. II only.
   c. I and III only.
   d. I, II, and III.

9. Harris notes that the use of forward rates for booking currency transactions is allowed in:
   a. The United States and many other countries.
   b. Many other countries but not the United States.
   c. The United States and only a few other countries.
   d. Neither the United States nor any other country.

10. According to Harris, a company's shareholders should treat exchange gains and losses:
    I. As being illusory for valuation purposes.
    II. As contributing real effects to the valuation process.
    III. With the normal valuation multiple used for the company.
    IV. With a more conservative valuation multiple than the multiple normally used.
    a. I only.
    b. II only.
    c. II and III only.
    d. II and IV only.

11. Harris illustrates that currency translation can and does affect a multinational company's:
    I. Balance sheet.
    II. Income statement.
    III. Cash flow statement.

a. I only.
b. II only.
c. I and II only.
d. I, II, and III.

12. According to Hawkins, the International Accounting Standards Committee (IASC) is likely to adopt the independent theory with respect to which of the following financial reporting issues:
a. Interim statements.
b. Segment accounting.
c. Pension obligations.
d. Asset impairments.

13. Hawkins contends that the IASC will require a company to write down an impaired asset when the company believes that the:
a. Asset impairment is permanent.
b. Present value of the future cash flows from the asset is less than the carrying value of the asset.
c. Asset can be disposed of at minimum loss.
d. Majority of the asset's original cost has been depreciated.

14. As a tool for reconciling accounting and taxable income, Schedule M-1 of Form 1120 involves which of the following activities:
   I. Adding to after-tax accounting net income items that are not deductible for tax purposes but are deductible for accounting purposes.
   II. Subtracting from after-tax accounting net income items that are deductible for tax purposes but are not deductible for accounting purposes.
a. I only.
b. II only.
c. Both I and II.
d. Neither I nor II.

15. According to Willens, what is the proper sequence of calculations to determine a company's gross deferred tax asset?
   I. Operating losses.
   II. Deductible temporary differences.
   III. Tax rate.
a. Add I and II; multiply the sum by III.
b. Subtract II from I; multiply the difference by III.
c. Multiply II by III; subtract the product from I.
d. Multiply I by III; add the product to II.

16. Which of the following accurately characterizes the phenomenon known as "trafficking in net operating losses (NOLs)" for acquisition purposes? The use of NOLs is:
a. Virtually unrestricted for both a buying company and a target company.
b. Severely restricted for both a buying company and a target company.
c. Virtually unrestricted for a target company, but severely restricted for a buying company.
d. Severely restricted for a target company, but virtually unrestricted for a buying company.

17. McConnell contends that the most important criterion for pooling-of-interests accounting pertains to:
a. Asset disposal.
b. Autonomy.
c. Stock reacquisition.
d. Voting common stock.

18. The "buy them up, break them up" mentality of some corporate acquirers is discouraged by the pooling-of-interests criterion pertaining to:
a. Stock reacquisition.
b. Autonomy.
c. Asset disposal.
d. Contingent payments.

19. Buyer Company has assets of $150, liabilities of $75, and equity of $75. Target Company has assets with a book value of $80 and a fair value of $100, liabilities of $30, and equity of $50. Buyer offers $150 in its own stock in exchange for Target's stock. Under purchase accounting, Buyer will record goodwill of:
a. $50.
b. $55.
c. $80.
d. $90.

20. According to McConnell, restructuring charges typically result from:
   I. Consolidation and/or relocation of operations.
   II. Abandonment of operations or productive assets.
   III. Impairment of carrying value of productive assets.
a. I only.
b. I and II only.
c. II and III only.
d. I, II, and III.

# Self-Evaluation Answers

1. d. Summarizing empirical evidence, Brownlee concludes that the relationship between earnings and stock returns has been historically weak and that earnings correlate more highly with stock returns in periods of business stability.

2. b. Brownlee argues that analysts and other external users would be better served by "business reporting," a concept advocated by the American Institute of Certified Public Accountants' 1994 report.

3. c. The subtleties of reporting earnings, believes Fridson, become clearer in the context of companies acting in the best interests of shareholders—in this case, by obtaining the cheapest capital possible.

4. b. Fridson uses the booking of earnings advances to illustrate the importance of timing considerations, not the power of underlying assumptions.

5. a. The ratios of accounts receivable and inventory to sales, especially unexpected changes therein, tend to be most helpful in detecting financial gimmicks.

6. d. In addition to depreciation and allowance for doubtful accounts, nonrecurring revenues, but not gross revenues, are a chief source of earnings manipulation.

7. d. Failing to mark securities to market is a common balance sheet manipulation, but it does not involve selling, general, and administrative expense.

8. d. Staley considers all three tasks to be important parts of the portfolio maintenance process.

9. b. Harris states that, contrary to U.S. practice, companies in many other countries are allowed to use forward rates in this context.

10. d. Harris contends that such gains and losses are indeed real to the shareholders but that the nonrecurring nature of the gains and losses probably calls for restraint in the valuation multiples used.

11. d. Harris provides convincing evidence that the traditional financial statements and, perhaps surprisingly to some observers, even the cash flow statement are affected, often dramatically, by the functional currency chosen and the translation approach used.

12. a. Hawkins believes that the IASC will require that statements for each interim period stand on their own, and will not allow companies to defer or allocate items that they could not defer or allocate in their annual periods.

13. b. The IASC, according to Hawkins, is moving toward a relatively quantifiable approach that reduces company discretion.

14. c. Willens details both steps in his discussion of Schedule M-1.

15. a. Willens states that the gross deferred tax asset is determined by multiplying the sum of operating losses and deductible temporary differences by the tax rate.

16. d. Willens points out that the tax law has long been asymmetrical in this regard, making companies with large NOLs much better acquirers than targets.

17. d. Although all four are criteria for pooling, McConnell argues that the requirement that the company offers and issues only voting common stock for 90 percent or more of the target's voting common stock is critical to the nature of pooling of interests.

18. c. According to McConnell, the 12th criterion for pooling of interests states that the combined corporation does not plan to dispose of a significant part of the combined assets within two years except in the ordinary course of business or to eliminate duplicate facilities.

19. c. McConnell's example shows that the purchase method would result in combined assets of $250, combined liabilities of $105, and combined equity of $225, implying a goodwill amount of $330 less $250, or $80.

20. d. McConnell notes that all three can and do give rise to restructuring charges.

# Selected Publications

## AIMR

*Economic Analysis for Investment Professionals,* 1997

*Global Equity Investing,* 1996

*Global Portfolio Management,* 1996
Jan R. Squires, CFA, *Editor*

*Implementing Global Equity Strategy: Spotlight on Asia,* 1997

*Investing in Small-Cap and Microcap Securities,* 1997

*Managing Endowment and Foundation Funds,* 1996

*Managing Investment Firms: People and Culture,* 1996
Jan R. Squires, CFA, *Editor*

*The Media Industry,* 1996

*Merck & Company: A Comprehensive Equity Valuation Analysis,* 1996
Randall S. Billingsley, CFA

*Risk Management,* 1996

*Standards of Practice Casebook,* 1996

*Standards of Practice Handbook,* 7th edition, 1996

*AIMR Performance Presentation Standards Handbook,* 2nd edition, 1997

## Research Foundation

*Company Performance and Measures of Value Added,* 1996
by Pamela P. Peterson, CFA, and David R. Peterson

*Currency Management: Concepts and Practices,* 1996
by Roger G. Clarke and Mark P. Kritzman, CFA

*Information Trading, Volatility, and Liquidity in Option Markets,* 1997
by Joseph A. Cherian and Anne Fremault Vila

*Initial Dividends and Implications for Investors,* 1997
by James W. Wansley, CFA, William R. Lane, CFA, and Phillip R. Daves

*Interest Rate and Currency Swaps: A Tutorial,* 1995
by Keith C. Brown, CFA, and Donald J. Smith

*Interest Rate Modeling and the Risk Premiums in Interest Rate Swaps,* 1997
Robert Brooks, CFA